Studying at a
distance

Studying at a distance

A guide for students

Christine J. Talbot

Open University Press
Maidenhead · Philadelphia

Open University Press
McGraw-Hill Education
McGraw-Hill House
Shoppenhangers Road
Maidenhead
Berkshire
England
SL6 2QL

email: enquiries@openup.co.uk
world wide web: www.openup.co.uk

and

325 Chestnut Street
Philadelphia, PA 19106, USA

First Published 2003

A catalogue record of this book is available from the British Library

ISBN 0 335 21336 7 (pb)   0 335 21337 5 (hb)

Library of Congress Cataloging-in-Publication Data
CIP data has been applied for

Typeset by RefineCatch Limited, Bungay, Suffolk
Printed in Great Britain by Bell and Bain Ltd, Glasgow

Contents

List of figures

Foreword

'Studying at a distance'? you may ask. What *is* 'distance learning'? And what about all the overlapping terms such as 'open learning', 'flexible learning', 'online learning' and 'independent learning' and so on? Distance learning may have its origins way back in the days of correspondence schools with a few learning providers who catered for students who for one reason or another did not want to, or were not able to, attend 'conventional' face to face education or training establishments. It could have been argued that to some extent in those days, distance learning was a substitute for 'real' learning, and that the writers of distance learning materials, alongside the tutors supporting learners at a distance, had the job of making distance learning as good as possible a substitute for traditional means of studying and gaining knowledge or qualifications.

Since distance learners were not in a position to learn together, or benefit from day to day contact with their teachers, they needed some help to learn at a distance, not least in how best to *manage* their learning and cope with learning in contexts where they had some freedom over the pace at which they learned. They needed help to handle the freedom of *where* they got down to their learning and *when* they chose to learn. They had the awesome responsibility of being, to some extent, *in charge* of their own learning and having to make the best they could of learning from resource materials without the normal amount of guidance from tutors, trainers or teachers. Not surprisingly, distance learners in these early times were thought to need quite a lot of help in fine-tuning their own approaches to learning so that they could help themselves to achieve the same sort of results which might be expected of 'normal' learners.

Strangely however, it was found gradually that many of the people who engaged in distance learning turned out to be perfectly successful learners. Indeed, many of the tutors and writers who got into distance learning also turned out to be successful at helping learning to happen, and in designing materials which lent themselves to people learning in their own ways, and at times, places and paces of their own choosing. More importantly, is was gradually realised that distance learning was much more than simply an alternative to 'normal' teaching and learning. Indeed, it was noticed that there were significant parallels between the processes of distance learning and conventional learning. Students on college-based programmes – the most successful students, more often than not – actually turned out to exercise a significant amount of control over their own learning, even in quite traditional teaching-learning environments. They did, in fact, choose learning strategies made up from tactics which built on making their own choices of how best to learn, and when and where to learn, and how fast to learn, and even (perish the thought) *what* to learn – and (dare we face this?) what *not* to learn. So-called 'normal' students were found to be eager for help, support and advice about how *best* to learn, even in institution-based learning contexts where they were surrounded by people who were learning the same things.

Meanwhile, it was noticed that people who successfully completed distance learning programmes had gained added value along the way. They had developed as *learners* at the same time as developing their knowledge or expertise in the subject matter involved. They were better able to manage their own future learning in whatever contexts they found themselves. They did not need teachers to the extent which may previously have been the case – they had moved towards being *independent* learners, or indeed *autonomous* learners. They had developed skills at *self-assessing* their learning along the way. They had equipped themselves with the skills and attributes which we would now associate with the most accomplished of *lifelong* learners. In short, they had changed the course of their lives. So distance learning became known to be not just a second-best option.

Concurrently, a revolution was taking place. Perhaps in future this will be looked back upon as the revolution of information and communications technologies, rivalling the invention of the printing press in the history of the growth in dissemination of information and knowledge. In a nutshell, it became a lot easier to package up information – and it became a lot *cheaper* to do so. As Einstein had observed decades before all of this happened, *information* did not automatically turn itself into knowledge however, and needed to be processed into *experience* for knowledge to result from having acquired it. In particular, however, the *electronic* aspects of this new revolution grew apace. Everything (for a while) had to have an 'e-'

in it to be up-to-date – e-learning, e-moderating, e-tutoring, not to mention e-fficient, e-ffective or e-clectic! However, the e-learning part of this revolution will only have reached its destination when we no longer talk about e-anything, but simply accept the electronic aspects of information and communication technologies as normal and unexceptional, and use the tools in the electronic toolkit in a 'fit for purpose' spirit for what they're good at, and no longer devise training days or write books about e-anything. And meanwhile, while information became cheaper to produce, the real costs of teaching and learning continued to rise – particularly those costs associated with the time spent by learners and teachers alike.

So distance learning had come of age. It turned out to be far too good just to be used for distance learners. College-based provision started to make much more use of learning at students' own pace. Students became expected to *manage* their choices of what to learn, when to learn it, how best to learn it, at what pace to learn it, and even with whom to learn it. 'Self-study pathways' were created so that students learned some things in distance learning mode, alongside other things that they learned in face to face mode. 'Independent-learning modules' were created. Indeed, some of these could also (surprise, surprise) be used by students who were not physically on campus – distance learners, in fact. Full circle?

This book *Studying at a Distance* could not be more timely. Distance learning is no longer an unknown quantity. There is abundant experience of how to support it. We now know a great deal more about how best to create distance learning resource materials. And above all, the 'distance' can now be real or imaginary. It can be practical or virtual. *Everyone* is now, at least to some extent, a distance learner, not least those who teach. All students now need to be more 'in charge' of their own learning. They all need guidance on how best to make the most of the plethora of learning resources they will encounter. They can all benefit from spending at least some of their time and energy becoming more skilled at the business of becoming effective and efficient *learners*.

This book arises from the author's experience and expertise which has grown alongside the development of the various aspects of distance learning, in a rich learning environment, at one particular higher education institution. Her wealth of experience at helping learners become *better* learners – and at the same time helping tutors become *better* tutors – shines throughout this book.

Focusing on the learning experience, rather than just on curriculum content, is also very timely. Nowadays, those who fund education talk in terms of 'widening participation', 'lifelong learning' and 'raising achievement' yet the spotlight remains on 'retention' – in other words ensuring that those who start out on learning pathways get to their respective destinations successfully. Meanwhile, the buzz word in the world of training is 'blended' – meaning (at its best) choosing fit-for-purpose processes for different learning pathways. This book should help many people get to their destinations, both directly and indirectly. It will help those who are supporting learners on distance learning or self-study elements, as well as those who are learning.

Above all, this book is written directly to learners – and by now you will appreciate that this does not just mean distance learners, but all who encounter elements of independent studying along their learning journeys. The language is friendly, supportive, informal and on-side with human beings who are purposefully learning – studying. Nor is there just advice: there are frequent quotes distilling into the book the wisdom and experience of countless people who have already embarked on distance learning journeys. And there are also Activities followed by Commentaries – allowing users of the book to exercise their own minds on particular aspects of distance learning, and then compare their thinking with wisdom gained from the hindsight and experience of others.

Like the best distance learning materials (whether print-based or electronic), this book unfolds in manageable chunks, and with a quite remarkable level of focusing in on what's really important. The first three chapters are to help learners get to grips with who they are, what they are preparing to face and the developments in technology which have become inseparable from distance learning. The next three chapters dig deep into the nuts and bolts of learning, the practicalities, the support aspects, and the diverse nature of the learning resources themselves. Next follows 'Making the most of your distance learning experience' – a chapter full of advice, help and practical realism, spanning working with others, reading, note making, essay writing, revision and exams. It is likely that many distance learners will use their skills regarding managing the time, place and pace of their learning, to home in on this chapter straightaway, as being the most central to their mission of becoming skilled at being an independent or autonomous learner, not just in the context of the particular modules or pathways they happen to be studying in distance learning mode, but by embracing other parts of their learning which may be in face to face or campus-based modes. Then finally, comes a chapter devoted to what, for many distance learners, is one of the greatest challenges they face – 'Doing your research project'.

Whether you're reading this book as a learner, as someone supporting learners, or someone managing learning environments, or as someone involved in designing and creating new learning resources, this book should help you to focus on what's important, making the processes and experiences of learning effective, efficient, enjoyable and – above all – *successful*. And by now, you will realise that this is not *just* about distance learning, but lifelong learning in all its forms – print-based, electronic, web-based, online and work-based.

Phil Race

at a distance. As with any distance learning course materials, if you work through the activities and think about the issues for yourself you will learn about them and retain the ideas far more effectively than if you just read passively about them. Ultimately, it is your choice how much benefit you derive both from this book and from your course materials.

This book includes quotes from comments and advice given by former students about their experience of studying by distance learning. The book is based on an original in-house version of the guide that was produced for distance learning students registered with the University of Leeds, UK, and the quotes are from former students of that university. The Leeds guide itself developed out of my experience of holding several enjoyable and informative preparatory sessions with University of Leeds distance learners attending face to face induction courses at the start of their distance learning courses.

The guide is not subject-specific and should prove useful to students registered on a distance learning course in any discipline. It is primarily intended to be used prior to beginning a course of study, though you may well return to it from time to time during your course as a source of encouragement or to look more closely at specific sections when they seem to be most relevant to your situation. This will be especially true of the 'Doing your research project' chapter.

I wish you well with your studies.

Christine Talbot

Acknowledgements

I should like to express my thanks to those course tutors and course administrators at the University of Leeds who collaborated in the collection of comments from students who have studied at a distance. I should also like to express my gratitude to the students themselves who were asked to share some of the difficulties they anticipated or actually encountered when studying, and the strategies they developed and specific steps they took to overcome those difficulties. They have contributed fully and frankly with their comments about their experiences (the positive and the not so positive) of learning at a distance, and many extracts from those comments are included in boxes scattered throughout this guide. Wherever possible I have contacted those students who I quote (anonymously) in the guide. Without exception, they generously have given me permission to do so.

I should also like to express my appreciation to the many colleagues at the University of Leeds who encouraged the production of the original guide and/or critically appraised earlier drafts of the material. In particular: Barbara Summers, Leeds University Business School; Cilla Ross, School of Continuing Education; Martin Wedell, School of Education; Pam Taylor, School of Medicine; Richard Hall and Siobhan Maguire, School of Mechanical Engineering; and Sue Baldwin, School of Healthcare Studies. Maggie Boyle, University of Leeds Skills Centre, and Rebecca O'Rourke, School of Continuing Education, University of Leeds, deserve special mention for their contributions to Chapter 7. My thanks also to Mark Clowes, Jane Saunders, Tracey Stanley, Adrian Smith and other colleagues in the University of Leeds Library for their significant contribution to Chapter 6 and Sections 8.2 and 8.3; and to Chris Butcher in the Staff and Departmental Development Unit at Leeds for his contribution to Chapter 2.

Chapter 8, 'Doing your research project', is based on research training materials prepared by me originally for postgraduate and research students at the University of Leeds. The original Leeds materials were reviewed by Margaret Orchard, Staff and Departmental Development Unit at Leeds, and Anne Fearful, formerly of Leeds University Business School and now at the University of St Andrews, Scotland. My thanks to both of them for their helpful comments.

For this Open University Press edition I have incorporated many amendments and improvements suggested by staff and students who have used the various editions of the Leeds version of the guide. I am grateful to them all for their contributions.

I should also like to express my appreciation to Alison Hughes and Debbie Prescott, University of Liverpool, and to Paul Chin, University of Hull, for reviewing the Leeds version of the guide; and to these and other colleagues in the Lancashire and Yorkshire network of Open, Distance and Flexible Learning Officers (ODFLOs) who have encouraged the production of this edition.

My grateful thanks to Tim May, of Salford University, for kind permission to reproduce his 'five stages at which values enter the research process' in Section 8.4 and to Professor Phil Race for writing the Foreword.

Thanks are also due to Chris Waterston, Leeds Metropolitan University, specifically for his contribution to the two mind maps in Chapter 7, but also for his constant support and patience during the many stages of writing this book.

Christine Talbot

Introduction

> 'Completing the course is a wonderful experience. Passing the [course] was one of the highlights of my life so far. I am able to analyse and use written information in a way that I could not do before. I am able to apply those skills to every aspect of my life.'

Studying at a distance

This guide is intended to help you to study by distance learning. Some of you using this guide may well be on a distance learning course that includes some elements of face to face contact with your tutors and fellow students, but you will largely be studying on your own, away from your college or university and from other people. Others may be following a 'hybrid' or 'mixed-mode' course that will include a combination of both face to face and distance study. You will therefore experience first hand the similarities and the differences between the two modes of study. Hundreds of thousands of people around the world have now successfully completed courses of study by both mixed and fully distance modes. However, it is acknowledged that studying at a distance can be a mixed blessing. The good news is that people perform at least as well studying as distance learners as they do studying face to face, and some people perform better – provided they finish the course.

Many find that the advantages of being able to progress at their own pace, where and when they choose to study, far outweigh the disadvantages associated with distance learning. Others have succeeded in spite of finding the studying heavy going, and still others have not completed their course because the problems have been too great. Many of those who have dropped out have said that the main reason for lack of success was that they just had not known what to expect and never quite came to terms with the demands placed upon them.

Purpose of the guide

This guide is meant to encourage you. It is also an attempt to provide you with the benefit of anticipating potential difficulties of studying at a distance, and with the opportunity to consider suggestions as to how to overcome them. It aims to reassure you that, with the right attitude and necessary commitment, you should succeed in the task ahead.

Studying at a distance for the first time brings with it its own sort of culture shock, since the differences between this and following a traditional face to face taught course can be significant. That said, there are many aspects of studying at a distance that are very similar to studying face to face. This guide incorporates numerous quotes (as in the box below) from those who have been there before you – and succeeded. Some voice the difficulties they encountered, reflecting the reality of their situation, and others also share the strategies employed to overcome those difficulties. Be encouraged!

> '. . . what a feeling when it is all finished, and you look back and see just what you have achieved. I know now the study . . . has widened my thought, knowledge and understanding, and given me confidence to develop opinions and contribute, even in areas less familiar.'

How to use the guide

The format of this guide introduces you to the style you may come across in the learning materials (whether in print or electronic form) provided by your module tutor. As I cannot be present with each of you as you work through this guide I have tried to anticipate some of your questions or reactions to what you read and have spelt out some things in detail. Inevitably things are included that you personally don't need, but others might. The beauty of such materials is that you can skip through those sections at your own pace without waiting for others to catch up with you. Conversely, there may be some parts with which you are unfamiliar and so find difficult. You can, in the privacy of your own home or workplace, re-read the material as many times as necessary until you grasp a particular idea – another typical characteristic of learning in this way, and the reason why some people perform better using the distance mode of delivery.

I have attempted to present the overall content of the book in a logical order. I appreciate, however, that for many of you some chapters will be more pertinent than others. Whilst I would strongly recommend that you work through Chapters 1 and 2 to begin with, there is no reason why, thereafter, you shouldn't use the guide in the order of chapters that best meets your own needs. (You will, however, find some degree of cross-referencing in the later chapters to content that has appeared earlier in the book.) For some of course there may be sections or even whole chapters that, after a quick skim, you will decide are unnecessary for you to read in detail because the content is already familiar to you.

Activities

Several self-study activities, some of which are followed by commentaries, have been included throughout the guide. You are strongly advised not to miss these out, as they are an essential part of the guide and introduce the crucial element of *active* (rather than *passive*) learning that is typical of studying at a distance. However, as I point out from time to time, it may be more appropriate for you to undertake some of the activities once you have started your course.

Response boxes

It is not possible to include full size blank boxes within this book for your responses to the activities. However, it is indicated at various points where it would be appropriate to note your response. I would suggest that you keep a separate notebook or computer file specifically for noting down all of your responses. You can then use this for easy reference whenever you refer back to this guide in the course of your studies.

What's included in the guide

After a brief look at reasons for studying and at goal setting you will identify the qualities needed to be an effective distance learner, the difficulties you are likely to encounter and the strategies available to help you to cope. You will also reflect on the qualities you already have. You will look at what studying and learning are, and at the ways in which distance learning is different. You are also given the opportunity to examine various approaches to learning and different styles of learning. You are then encouraged to get to know yourself better as a learner, and to work out the details of how, where and when you are going to study.

You are introduced to the various elements of e-learning that you may be expected to use on your course. Suggestions are offered about getting support during your studies and about the various resources available to you for studying. For those of you who will have to engage in a significant project and to write some form of report or dissertation, you will find the chapter on doing a research project helpful. There is also a chapter on making the most of your distance learning experience for those of you who need something of a refresher regarding some basic study skills. There is a section at the start of that chapter on working with others when studying at a distance for those of you who have not had much experience of working collaboratively with other students before. Finally a checklist of all of the information you need to obtain in advance about your course is provided and suggestions made about where you might find it.

What's not included

Although this guide does contain some information on developing your reading skills and with making notes, writing essays and sitting examinations some of you may require more detailed guidance. There are many excellent books and other resources available that provide this, and the final section of this guide (Further Resources) contains details of other resources (paper and electronic) that can help you further develop such skills, should you need to do so.

Whilst there is a chapter on doing your research project, this chapter does not attempt to provide everything you need to know about doing research, but there are many excellent and comprehensive books available to help you. Some of these are included in the Further Resources and References sections at the end of this book. In particular the chapter does not look at specific methodologies or techniques for actually doing the research. Rather it is an attempt to provide the practical framework within which you will need to work to successfully conduct and report on your research.

This guide does not provide specific information about your course: the course handbook or student handbook provided by the institution where you register for your course will do that.

You belong to your institution

Remember as you work through this guide that, once you are registered for a specific course, you are a bona fide student member of your study institution. As such you are just as entitled to the provision of services and support as any other student. Whilst the form of those services and support may differ from those provided for on-campus students, they should be equivalent.

A note on terminology

The terms 'course' and 'module', and 'course' and 'programme' have been used interchangeably in the guide since different terms are used in different institutions. In general the term 'programme' is used to mean a whole series of smaller units of study, such as, say, six 20-credit modules.

I am confident that all of you using this guide will find much to support and encourage you in your studies.

1 Preparing for the task ahead

Distance learning often requires of the student a degree of initiative and mental resilience not always associated with learning in a classroom with a peer group and a teacher in attendance . . . Learning alone can be difficult, despite encouragement from friendly tutors, especially if you are not accustomed to studying.

[Philpot 1997]

Introduction

There are many issues that it is good to consider *before* you actually start your course. Doing this helps you to get things clear in your head, be more organised and generally feel far more prepared to begin studying. In this chapter you will look at your own reasons for studying and at what your goals are for your course. You will then look in greater detail at how you can be an effective distance learner.

> '. . . getting back into the academic world after years of earning a living . . . has been like a breath of fresh air . . . For anyone who went to University but, like me, wasted a lot of their time (even if they had a good time wasting it!), distance learning is a great opportunity to do the things I should have done, or forgot to do.'

1.1 Why are you studying?

This might seem a strange question at first, but it is important for you to be quite clear why you have made your commitment to study. When the going gets tough, it is helpful to remind yourself of your reasons for starting studying and why these reasons are important to you. It's not very wise to start a course because someone else wants you to do it – *you* have to put in the hard work, not them, so you must want to do it for your own sake.

> 'Be sure of the reasons why you are undertaking the course. I had to be sure that my motivation would last the two years the [course] took to complete.'

Activity One

Note briefly *your* reasons for wanting to begin (and complete!) your course of study.

> *Note your response*

Commentary

Clearly your answers are specific to you, but there are usually certain themes in the reasons people specify. For some people the reasons are related to their present job or their career aspirations, for others it is a personal ambition to study for a particular level of qualification, and for others it is a more general desire for personal development, including 'improving the mind'. Whatever *your* reasons, it is important to keep these in mind for those off days that we all have. Your reasons may well change as you progress in your studies but it's important to be sure of what they are now, to give you the motivation that you need.

1.2 Motivation / goal setting

Self-motivation isn't always easy – you need to have goals to provide a driving force. As well as knowing *why* you want to study, effective learning also depends upon your knowing *what* it is you want to study. You are probably using this guide after enrolling on your course of study, but you may yet have to make decisions about which non-compulsory modules you are going to study. Although your ideas may only evolve as you work through the earlier parts of the course, you probably have an overall idea of the knowledge and skills you would like to possess by the end of your studies.

Activity Two

Take a few minutes now to note down what knowledge and skills you want to develop by the end of the course.

Note your response

Commentary

Returning to this list from time to time may help boost your motivation when it is flagging, by refocusing on your goals and providing you with direction. It is also possible that you will need to re-set your goals for studying on, say, a three- or six-monthly basis. You may also need to re-set your broader lifestyle goals in the light of experience, especially with regard to the balance between work, study and relaxation. (We will consider this in more detail in Chapter 4.)

'Despite the difficulties, I enjoyed studying at a distance. I now have the confidence to work independently and can explore my own subject matter in a systematic, logical way.'

1.3 What qualities do you need to be an effective distance learner?

Activity Three

Make a note of those personal attributes and skills that you think you need if you are successfully to complete your distance learning course. Two suggestions are:

- Motivation
- Initiative

Note your response

'I could go up to 6 weeks and not have to be physically present for lectures – I found it hard to be disciplined enough to keep working in between taught sessions.'

'I found that I was disciplined, as I knew I would be penalised for failing to meet deadlines.'

Commentary

Many personal attributes and skills needed for studying at a distance are the same as those required by any other learner, but some take on greater significance when learning at a distance. The following have been suggested by students who have attended face to face sessions on studying at distance:

- Self-confidence
- Perseverance / resilience
- Determination
- Self-discipline
- Time management skills

- Forward planning
- Effective communication skills
- Ability to take responsibility for your learning
- A balanced learning style
- Critical reading and note making skills
- IT skills
- Information retrieval skills
- Effective record-keeping
- The ability to ask for help from the most appropriate source

You may well have thought of others. As you work through this guide there is the opportunity for you to look at some of the attributes in the above list and to consider suggestions offered on how to acquire or develop any of those that you feel you do not yet have.

'The light at the end of the tunnel is a great motivational factor (and the one that has kept me going), whether the course is for a job related qualification which will achieve promotion, advancement or a pay-rise!, or even just the personal satisfaction and pride that completion will bring.'

'I feel self-directed learning also means asking for help when you need it, rather than working in isolation.'

1.4 Potential pitfalls and how to avoid them

This section is, in some ways, complementary to the previous one. Even with all or most of the qualities specified above it is likely that you will have obstacles to effective learning that need to be overcome. It might seem a rather negative approach to take, but unless you acknowledge potential problems you cannot take evasive action or prepare yourself to solve those problems that cannot be avoided. Almost everyone faces difficulties in starting a distance learning course, so you are not alone. Some problems are common to lots of students, but some may be specific to you.

Activity Four

In the light of what you have read so far, what difficulties do you expect to have to deal with if you are successfully to complete your distance learning course? Some of them are likely to relate to your personal / life circumstances (for example, domestic responsibilities) and others to the actual process of studying and learning (for example, writing essays).

Note your response

'Before commencing on my distance learning course with the university, I had a number of unfounded fears (now I look back on the experience). I wondered if I would fit in, think quickly enough, and whether the breadth of my experience would be wide enough to contribute to the topics being studied. I wondered if I would find the tutors would talk in an academic language I would not understand. Other fears I had included my ability to be organised and keep to a study programme and have my assignment in on time.'

Commentary

You may have included some of the following:

Personal / life circumstances

- Coping with the conflicting demands of studying, work and home life
- Getting away from home / work for the residentials
- Not being supported practically or emotionally by family / friends / work colleaques
- Cost of travel and overnight accommodation

Studying and learning

- Finding time to study

- Having the confidence to start studying again after many years
- Writing essays again
- Coping with stress at the time of the examinations
- Being motivated enough to persevere when not attending university or college on a regular basis
- Feeling isolated because of not seeing fellow students regularly
- Feeling disheartened or unsure of progress because of not seeing the tutor regularly
- Keeping a balance between the work required for the face to face and distance learning elements of the course (if on a mixed-mode course)
- Not having the self-discipline to get down to doing the work
- Finding somewhere quiet to work
- Finding the level of the course too high to be able to complete it
- Coping with learning a whole new vocabulary relevant to the course
- Using the Internet to communicate with others and submit assignments
- Working / learning according to the rules of a different academic / educational culture

> 'Just concentrate on one thing at a time. Distance learning does not mean isolation. A small group of students exchanged telephone numbers, e-mail addresses, and we did use them to contact each other regularly. At the height of the loneliness of the dissertation, I was in contact with one friend every day.'

It is quite normal for students new to learning at a distance to have some anxiety about doing so. It could even be seen as a good thing, since the desire to overcome the anxiety might provide the motivation that you need to begin. It is good to acknowledge fears about learning if those fears (and often misconceptions about learning) are to be lessened. However, too much anxiety is not helpful to positive learning. If you have serious worries about the whole process it would be wise to get in touch with the course tutor to talk things through sooner rather than later. Hopefully though, you will feel better prepared for the experience once you have worked through this guide.

> 'Take regular breaks, keep up physical activity and arrange to see friends and go out occasionally. It is important to look after yourself, but still retain a focus and determination to complete the study healthily and in one piece.'

We will be looking at issues of time management and sources of support, in Section 4.6 and Chapter 5 respectively, to help overcome some of your anticipated difficulties. Even when studying at a distance it is possible to put support mechanisms in place and many of these are likely to have been anticipated by your course tutor. Chapter 7 provides you with a refresher in basic study skills and, as mentioned in the Introduction to this guide, there are some further excellent guides to the process of studying and completing assignments, sitting exams and so on, listed in Further Resources at the end of this book. By the time you use this guide you will have probably already been accepted onto a course. This means that your tutors believe that you *will* be able to succeed in your studies, so once again – be encouraged.

Demands on you

> 'I miss lectures where I can hear others' comments and questions and realise that I am not alone in missing the point. I do not enjoy studying in a bubble.'

No one finds it easy when they first enter a new field (in studying or at work) or move into a higher level in a familiar field. Hopefully your course material will ease you in gently and get the brain going again. Many course materials include a glossary of new terms and a list of abbreviations and acronyms, so that you can turn to these as many times as you need until new vocabulary has 'sunk in'. If there isn't such a glossary it is probably a good idea to create your own, adding new terms and their definitions as you come across them.

There is, however, no escaping the fact that studying is hard work and you need to be fully committed to the whole process. But you mustn't let it take over your whole life. What is potentially a rewarding and enjoyable experience can easily become only a chore if you don't maintain a healthy balance between studying and other aspects of your life.

> Difficulty: 'Balancing work, home, family and studying commitments.'
>
> Strategy: 'Prioritising and planning, i.e. day for studying; day for time with family (important to keep everything in balance).'

If you decide that you are taking a day off with no studying and no work, then do it and don't feel guilty, otherwise you will not feel the benefit. Likewise if you set aside a time for studying, worrying that the grass needs cutting will be counter-productive. This might make it sound as though every day you plan as a study day will be a very positive experience and very productive but, of course, this isn't always the case. We all have our 'off' days when no amount of perseverance will help us learn anything. Although you need the self-discipline, it might occasionally be as well to cut your losses and go off and do something completely different – you will probably come back refreshed and ready to learn after all. Beware of too many 'off' days though – if this starts to happen too frequently, you may need to talk things over with your tutor.

> 'Don't forget home / family / friends. They also need to be timetabled and don't feel guilty for giving them time.'

Demands on others

> 'You need a supportive partner who can listen to tales of hardship and woe. My wife had to get used to me disappearing upstairs to work. When we had days off together I often had to work at an essay. Distance learning can impose a strain on partners that may be unappreciated by the student who is worrying about an essay reference list.'

There is no doubt that any form of studying, and distance learning in particular, makes demands on those around you – at home, at work and at play. Only you can judge how interested and supportive your family, colleagues and friends are likely to be, and the degree to which you should discuss your studies with them. Embarking on a new course of study might be very important to you at the moment, but others may see things differently.

> 'Don't expect other people to automatically understand what you are doing the course for. It may even be difficult for you to explain it to them. I had an underlying conviction that this is what I wanted to do.'

Practical issues such as a quiet place to study or time to do so have to be resolved by you and those you live and work with. Most people find that if they set out what they are going to need and when they are going to need it clearly but firmly in advance, their 'demands' are better received than if they make them aggressively and expect instant response. Asking for the TV to be switched off 'now' so that you can have peace and quiet for studying, or wanting to take time off work for studying 'today', understandably won't make you popular with most people. The best advice is simply to keep the channels of communication open – keep people informed.

1.5 Experience counts

Whether you have recently finished a course of study or are returning to study for the first time in many years, you will already possess many skills needed to be a successful distance learner. Many of the skills outlined in the Commentary to Activity Three are acquired simply through life's experiences. Your earlier studies and work situations will have been valuable training grounds. In addition to learning skills, as an adult learner you will bring other relevant skills, knowledge and experiences, opinions and ideas to your studies. Although there will be new knowledge, understanding and skills to acquire, your main task will be to fit these into your existing ways of thinking. This will result in your reassessing and possibly revising some of your current views, but the learning process will be an enriching one for you. (You will explore the learning process more fully in Chapter 2.) Although studying at a distance is challenging, you almost certainly already possess what is needed to have a very positive learning experience.

Summary of Chapter 1

In this chapter you have:

- Considered why you are studying
- Thought about what it is you want to achieve by following this course
- Identified the qualities you need to be an effective distance learner
- Recognised that there will be difficulties ahead
- Begun to consider what strategies to put in place to cope with the demands that studying is likely to make upon you and those around you
- Received reassurance that you can do this

The key to success is getting to know yourself as a learner, making the most of what you have and knowing how to acquire what you need. This, essentially, is what the whole of this guide is about. The process begins in the next chapter in which you are encouraged to get to know yourself better as a learner.

2   Know yourself as a learner

Distance education is based on the premise that students are at the center of the learning process, take responsibility for their own learning, and work at their own pace and in their own place. It is about ownership and autonomy.

[Wheeler 1999]

Introduction

This chapter provides a structure by which you can carry out some self-reflection about yourself as a learner. You will find that taking time to work through the chapter will be time well spent. First you will consider what learning actually is and the characteristics of distance learning. This will be followed by a consideration of what your sources of learning will be. You will then look in some detail at the learning process and at the different approaches people take to learning. Finally you will be encouraged to explore your own learning preferences.

2.1 What is studying?

This can simply be described as the process by which you learn.

The aim of any studying must surely be that you, the student, are able to learn effectively. Although studying is hard work, you will hopefully also be able to enjoy your learning experience. Learning has its own intrinsic rewards, potentially bringing you enormous satisfaction. There are the extrinsic rewards too: perhaps a new job is on the horizon, or promotion within your present job.

2.2 What is learning?

Learning is essentially the acquisition of new skills, knowledge and attitudes, and the recognition of how they relate to the skills, knowledge and attitudes you already possess. But learning is also the process of understanding what has been acquired, and applying it to both familiar and new situations. As Karen Rawlins (1996) suggests 'learning is a process of self development' (p. 21) and 'students learn most effectively by relating knowledge to previous and current experience' (p. 20).

2.3 What will you learn?

What you will learn will be determined by the syllabus for your particular course. A syllabus, however, whilst providing a useful list of topics to be covered within a course or a specific module of a course, does not spell out in detail exactly what a student should be capable of by the end of the course. In most further and higher education institutions, in order for a course to gain official approval, these capabilities have to be expressed in the form of a set of learning outcomes. This is not a new concept, but the use of learning outcomes has increased in recent years.

Bloom *et al.* (1956) classified the outcomes of learning into three areas or domains:

1 **Psychomotor** to do with skills.
2 **Cognitive** to do with thinking abilities: comprehending / understanding information, that is, what we know and what we do with what we know.
3 **Affective** to do with attitudes and approaches.

Within each of these domains we can identify a number of stages that can be viewed in a hierarchical way. Since your learning will be largely to do with the cognitive domain we will look at that first, in some detail. The outcomes of *cognitive* learning can be categorised under a number of headings, in terms of what the learner can do, from the lowest level (knowledge) to the highest level (evaluation):

1	**Knowledge**	can recall what has been learned.
2	**Comprehension**	can recall what has been learned and it has significance.
3	**Application**	can apply what has been learned in a familiar or a novel situation.
4	**Analysis**	can tease out the threads of meaning from a range of information.
5	**Synthesis**	can weave the threads together in a new way.
6	**Evaluation**	can judge the significance and value of what has been learned.

Generally speaking, the higher the level of course you are taking, the higher the level of learning outcome (as defined by Bloom *et al.*) you will be expected to demonstrate, but any course should expect you to go well beyond memorising facts and being able to recall them. Assessment on any course is essentially the measurement of the extent to which you have achieved the learning outcomes for that course. A minimum requirement in any assessment will be that you can demonstrate that you have understood the knowledge you have acquired, and most courses will expect you to be able to apply that understanding of knowledge to a situation that is new to you, or to your existing situation in new ways.

Similarly hierarchies can be constructed for the affective and psychomotor domains. For the *affective* domain the range would be from:

1 Not realising / being unaware of an attitude, approach or value, through
2 Being conscious of not having this attitude, approach or value, through to
3 Adopting the attitude, approach or value, and it eventually becoming a part of your everyday response.

The critical approach to reading or the problem solving approach in science and medicine serve as useful examples. The affective domain can also be described as someone's attitude or approach developing from being:

1   Unconscious Incompetent to
2   Conscious Incompetent to
3   Conscious Competent to
4   Unconscious Competent.

In each instance the attitude of the student develops from one of total acceptance that facts are true, through the stage where uncertainty is beginning to creep in, until eventually everything is automatically questioned and alternatives are sought or created.

For the *psychomotor* domain we can consider a spectrum of expertise for students. The range would be from:

1   Being unable to do something, through
2   Doing something with a set of instructions, to
3   Doing something without instructions, to
4   Devising new ways of doing something and giving
    instructions to others.

> 'The university is more interested in analysis and synthesis than descriptive accounts that demonstrate a wide but superficial knowledge base.'

Although Bloom *et al.* defined these categories and levels nearly 50 years ago, they are still regarded by many, myself included, as a useful tool with which the objectives of learning can be made clear for teachers, students and examiners. Always check what the learning outcomes are for each part of your course before you start. Since assessment will be linked to the learning outcomes, knowing the learning outcomes will help you to know what you are working towards during your studies.

2.4 Characteristics of distance learning

At first glance the characteristics listed in the sub-headings in this section do not appear to be exclusive to distance learning, but will be present in all effective learning. However, as described in each paragraph, each characteristic takes on a greater significance, and is made possible in a distinct way, in distance learning.

Learning by doing

Good distance learning involves active learning. You will be asked to complete activities or tasks that are built into the learning materials. These are the equivalent of activities or tasks completed in the classroom. You may also be asked to contribute to a web-based discussion group. This is the equivalent of making a contribution to a group discussion in the classroom.

Learning by assessment

You may be asked to complete self-assessment questions (SAQs). These are the equivalent of doing short, regular tests in the classroom. The results of the tests don't count towards your final mark for each module, the answers are usually provided for you and it is a way of checking on your own progress. They can also be used by a group of students in a local study group to share issues about progress on particular topics with their peers (fellow students).

By completing SAQs, checking your progress and reading feedback, you are likely to perform much better on those assignments that do count towards your final mark. It is a very pragmatic approach to learning.

Other forms of so-called 'formative' assessment may also be included. Formative assessment is assessment that occurs during learning to inform and direct learning. It provides feedback to you about progression towards a goal or standard. It may carry marks, but the principal purpose is development rather than judgement.

Learning by reading feedback

Feedback may be incorporated into the original learning materials, written by the author of the module in anticipation of your responses to activities or SAQs, or it may be written by your tutor in response to assignments you have submitted in the course of studying the module. The assignments may or may not count towards your final mark for the module, but either way the feedback is provided to enhance your learning. Perhaps it will give you ideas about how you could have improved upon your answers, and perhaps it will give you pointers as to what you need to concentrate on before the final assignment is due. Good feedback will include not just the 'right' answers (indeed in many cases there is no such thing) but suggestions as to why certain responses would be appropriate and others would not. Feedback can also provide you with something very positive: what is good about your work and in what ways your work has improved.

Learner autonomy – taking control of and responsibility for your learning

One of the most significant differences between distance learning and conventional courses is that you have to take far more responsibility. Because distance learning is centred on you, the student, you have to make a lot more decisions. Although the course and module leaders will set targets (for example, assignments to complete or seminars to attend) you will be organising your own study timetable between those, and balancing your study with the rest of your life. You will, to a large degree, have control over the time, place and pace of studying and, perhaps to a lesser degree, be able to choose the materials that you use to study. You may also have some say in the nature, frequency and timing of assessments and as to where the assessments are completed. But with this control comes responsibility. You will have to ensure that your work and assignments are completed according to the schedule you have set out. (See Section 4.6 for suggestions about a study schedule and a weekly planner.)

Learning by reflection

You are more likely to take control of your learning if you build in time to regularly reflect during your learning. Think about what you have read, what was discussed in a group tutorial, your own ideas as they develop, your achievement during a practical session, and the progress (or lack of it) that you feel you are making.

> 'Keeping a reflective diary was a lifesaver too, it helped with keeping a focus on the tutorials and kept a perspective overall to refer to for support and contemplation. Reflecting on the contents, a clear direction and sense of 'moving on' emerged.'

2.5 Sources of learning

You will employ a number of strategies to help yourself learn, but I suggest that you pause to consider at this point the ways in which you will access information from which to learn. In the face to face taught situation your tutor is largely responsible for providing access to information, through lecturing or demonstrating, but most students following a course on campus are also likely to have to find sources for themselves at various stages in their studies.

Activity Five

List the various ways in which you, as a distance learner, are likely to access information for learning. Two suggestions are:

- By reading the learning materials provided in workbooks, study packs, etc.
- By observing someone at work, on the television or on video perform a task

Note your response

Commentary

In addition to the two ways suggested above, you will probably have included some of the following:

- By reading books and articles found by searching library resources
- By accessing information on a CD-ROM or via the Internet
- By accessing information from professional associations
- By discussing subjects with other students, either face to face or via the Internet
- By discussing subjects with your tutors, either face to face or via email
- By examining a picture or diagram on paper

- By examining a painting, drawing or sculpture in an art gallery or exhibition
- By listening to someone in person, on the radio or on audiotape explain various concepts or procedures, or speak a language you are learning
- By listening to music at a concert, on the TV / radio, or on a tape or CD
- By going to a play or ballet at the theatre
- By thinking something through and considering all of the options based on present knowledge and making an educated guess about what might be the result of certain actions
- By attempting problem solving, that is trying something out to see if it works and revising the method in the light of the results
- By reading recommended textbooks, details of which are provided by your course or module tutor(s)

Some of the above are clearly more relevant to some subjects than to others. As you will learn in Section 2.8 we all have preferences for the ways in which we like to learn, so you may not have included some of the above.

We will look in more detail at resources for studying in Chapter 6.

Author's note

The following three sections (2.6, 2.7 and 2.8) look further at the learning process, approaches to learning, and at learning preferences. The response by previous users of this guide to these sections has varied. Some people clearly take a greater interest in the process of learning than others do. If you do not wish to go into this depth of analysis about learning at this point, simply skip forward to Chapter 3. You may decide to return to the skipped sections later.

In the Appendix you will find a brief summary of types of education (for example, andragogy and pedagogy) and of open, distance, flexible and self-directed learning. This may be of interest to some of you using this guide.

2.6 The learning process

The Experiential Learning Cycle

What you do with information once you have accessed it is crucial. Learning is a continual process and it is *not* a passive process. We remember 10 percent of all we hear, 50 percent of all we see and 90 percent of all we do. The figures seem to vary in different versions of this brief maxim, but the message is always the same: we learn best by doing, by experience. Good distance learning materials will encourage active learning.

Nor does learning happen in straight lines, that is, it is not just a simple process of going through a few stages from beginning to end and finishing, and *hey presto* the learning is complete. Rather it has been likened to a cycle or a spiral.

Kolb combined these two concepts of experiential learning and cyclical learning in his four-stage Experiential Learning Cycle (Kolb 1984). The cycle moves through 'active experimentation', 'concrete experience', 'reflective observation' and 'abstract conceptualization' (p. 42). This cycle has been adapted many times by many people. My own interpretation of it, which I have found to be useful in a higher education setting, is shown in Figure 2.1.

The stages are more clear-cut in a scientific experimental setting, but the process is equally applicable to the arts, humanities and social

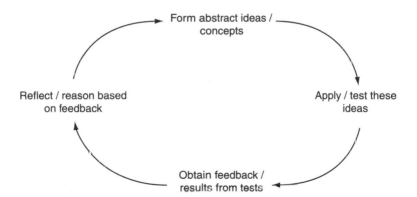

Figure 2.1 Continuous Learning Cycle
Source: loosely adapted from Kolb (1984)

sciences. An *abstract idea* cannot be fully absorbed or internalised until it has been *applied* in some way and objective *feedback* received on its application. This will involve some sort of *activity*, even if only talking the idea through with a tutor or fellow student. Having obtained the feedback on your idea you are likely to *reflect* on it, refine that *idea* and *test* it out again. Any reflection will be affected by other learning experiences that are stored in the memory. The feedback sometimes will come via an internal process, for example by your own reading – it doesn't always depend upon receiving feedback directly from others.

Learning may begin at any point in the cycle – you might have thought a lot before participating in an activity, or you might just launch yourself straight into something – and you are likely to go round the cycle many times before a particular concept or idea is fully learned. Even then, you may return to that particular learning cycle some time in the future and go round a few more times to refine or develop your learning. You may start at the reflection stage, having heard about someone else's activity and its outcomes, or you may observe or be part of someone else's test and draw your own conclusions from that learning experience. These conclusions may lead you to formulate your own ideas that you then test out. The movement round the cycle may not be smooth and the length of time it takes to move from one stage to the next will vary considerably from one person to another and for the same person in different learning situations. What is important is that you complete the full cycle and do not simply stick at one particular point, having completed only one or two stages in the cycle. (Honey and Mumford ([1982] 1992) adapted Kolb's cycle to use as the basis for their Learning Styles Questionnaire, which we will look at in Section 2.8.)

Reflection is an essential element of learning. If we make mistakes or indeed if we succeed, we need to reflect on that experience so that we know either how to avoid making the same mistakes again (where we have been unsuccessful) or to ensure that we repeat the process (where we have succeeded). Even before learning begins it is possible to reflect on the learning process itself (as outlined above) and to consider what skills and attributes you already possess and can bring to the process and which ones you need to acquire. It is also worthwhile considering the potential problems you might face in learning at a distance. (You were encouraged to do both of these in Chapter 1.)

2.7 Approaches to learning

As well as recognising that you need to complete the full learning cycle it will be useful for you to recognise that students adopt various approaches to learning. Although it is beyond the scope of this short guide to include a comprehensive survey of the research in this area, you might find it useful to acknowledge the approach that you are inclined to take. You might want to attempt to adjust that approach if you consider that any change is necessary.

Surface and deep learning

Two approaches to learning that have long been recognised are termed *surface* and *deep* learning (Marton and Saljö 1976). They represent the extremes of a continuum. At one end a student's learning is orientated to rote learning: the intention is memorisation and the focus is upon trying to learn elements of content 'off-by-heart'. At the other extreme a student's learning is orientated to comprehension: the intention is understanding and the focus is on the content as a whole, its structure and meaning, and on connections between different elements.

The approach that you take will depend upon your concepts of learning, and the learning environment (the type of task, the workload, the intellectual demand, the quality and quantity of support from staff, and so on) that you are in. Clearly the approach that will lead to a better quality of learning is the deep approach. The danger of the surface approach is that you will not be able to use what you have learned because you have not really understood it, you will simply be able to restate it. Having a deeper approach to learning is more likely to make the subject more interesting and enjoyable and to make it of more use to you. That said, there might be times when you decide (knowingly) to take a surface approach to learning because it is more practical to do so. Such a decision could well be part of a third approach to learning.

Strategic learning

Entwistle and Ramsden (1983) identified the *strategic* (achieving orientation) approach to learning. The student taking this approach aims to gain the highest grades and looks for ways to achieve this. This student is also balancing the demands of all of his / her courses (and / or work and family / social life) and making choices about best use of time and effort. It depends how one interprets the characteristics of this approach as to whether one admires or deplores it. (It has to be said that, in order to get through my day I need to be strategic about my workload and prioritise those tasks that are going to be most productive / rewarding and / or that the boss is demanding!)

'The course team sent us a lot of distance learning material. I only read what I had to in order to find an essay title and complete the assignment. I did not have time to read it all. However, now I have finished the course, I have gone back to the material and used it at work.'

The decision about *your* approach to learning (and the responsibility for that decision) has to be yours.

2.8 How do you prefer to learn?

Just as we differ in our *approach* to learning, we all have preferences about *how* we learn. There are several alternatives to analysing this: two that students have found helpful are detailed below.

Learning Styles Questionnaire

One is the Honey and Mumford ([1982] 1992) Learning Styles Questionnaire and the four learning styles the authors have identified: *activist, reflector, theorist* and *pragmatist*. Their analysis is loosely based on Kolb's learning cycle. They suggest that the four styles of learning are associated with particular stages in the learning cycle. If, for example, your preferred style is that of activist, you are more likely to feel comfortable at Kolb's stage of 'concrete experience'. In practice, most people show a preference for at least two of the styles. However, since the aim is to complete the full learning cycle it follows that we should also aim to develop all four styles of learning if we are to fully benefit from all aspects of learning.

Activity Six

The Learning Styles Questionnaire and how to score it is available in Honey and Mumford's ([1982] 1992) *The Manual of Learning Styles*. It is also available *for a fee* on Peter Honey's website (see Study guides on the web in the Further Resources section at the end of this book for details). It is well worth completing it in order to get to know your preferred learning style. General descriptions of the four styles and suggestions for using the results to improve your learning are also included in the book and on the website.

Commentary

Very few people are all-round learners, so don't be surprised if you score high on one or other scale. The results will indicate those situations in which you will function best and those in which you are likely to perform less well. If you have any choice in the matter, you can select those learning experiences that suit you best, but there are also some suggestions included in Honey and Mumford (1995) as to how you might develop further those areas where you are less strong, so that you can benefit from all kinds of learning.

The VARK Questionnaire

The VARK Questionnaire developed by Neil Fleming, New Zealand, and Charles Bonwell, USA, enables you to discover (or confirm) your learning preferences:

> V = visual graphic, i.e. pictures
> A = aural/ auditory
> R = visual text, i.e. reading
> K = kinesthetic, i.e. using all of the senses of sight, touch, taste, smell and hearing
>
> MM = multimodal

A website has been developed from where it is possible to complete the VARK Questionnaire interactively. (For more details see Study guides on the web in Further Resources.)

Summary of Chapter 2

In this chapter you have:

- Considered what learning is and how some aspects of learning are particularly significant in distance education
- Created your own list of sources of learning
- Looked at learning as a cyclical process
- Been introduced to different approaches to learning and to different learning styles
- Reflected upon your own learning preferences

3   E-learning

'The most important factor – get a computer and learn how to email and use [the] Internet.'

Introduction

Although access to and the use of personal computers (PCs) at home and at work is rapidly increasing, still not everyone makes regular use of a computer. Even if you do use a computer at work, the way in which you are expected to use one as a student may differ from what you are used to. There are increasingly elements of e-learning, or learning electronically, in most programmes of study in higher education. In this chapter you will explore the implications of that for your studies.

3.1 What do we mean by e-learning?

Activity Seven

List those things that you consider come under the heading of e-learning.

Note your response

Commentary

You may well have included some of the following:

- Using computers for learning
- Online learning
- Learning on the Net / Internet
- Web-based learning
- Learning using web pages
- WWW (World Wide Web, the web)
- The virtual (not real) classroom
- Learning via a virtual learning environment (VLE, also ELE / MLE)
- CD-ROM learning
- Computer-based learning
- Emailing
- Using mailing lists
- Conferencing boards
- Discussion rooms
- One to one chat

All of the above (and more!) are elements of e-learning. You will see from the list above that *online* learning is one type of e-learning. However, not all e-learning is online learning, that is you do not need to be connected live to the Internet for all e-learning – you may receive CD-ROM or floppy discs with files or programs on them, which you can use on your own PC.

You are increasingly likely to be expected to engage in some aspect of e-learning during your distance learning course, if only to communicate with your tutor by email occasionally. The information provided by your department before you registered as a student should have indicated if there would be any elements of e-learning on your course. More detailed information is likely to be provided as the course progresses. You should also receive information about the specification for *hardware* (that is, computer / printer / modem, and so on) required, and about which versions of *software* (that is, computer programs / version of Windows, and so on) you will need to install on your computer to enable you to access the materials they will provide.

Activity Eight

It is very frustrating once the course has started to find that you do not have the required hardware or software to use files sent to you on disc or to access information on the web when asked to do so. It is recommended that at this point you find any documentation already received about this and check that your hardware and software are up to the required standards. A university or college help-desk is usually available to provide advice on how to access new software, much of which is free to download from the Internet.

3.2 Accessibility of e-learning materials

Legislation in the UK makes it illegal to refuse to serve, offer a lower standard of service or offer a service on worse terms to a disabled student. This means that if a disabled student finds it unreasonably difficult to use a service, an educational institution has to make reasonable changes to that service. Examples of these services include departmental, faculty and institutional websites, intranets, virtual learning environments (such as *Blackboard* or *WebCT*) and other resources – not just electronic / digital. This means that learning materials (in whatever form) must be provided in a suitable format to be accessible to all students. Please contact your programme leader if you need any of the course materials in a different format to that provided as standard.

3.3 Glossary of terms

Many of you will already be very familiar with much of the terminology used when working with computers, but if you're not it would be worth reading through the terms in Figure 3.1 to ensure that you are clear about their meanings. No doubt within the next year or two there will be several more terms in common use. Some of the types of e-learning will be explored in more detail in the following pages.

Broadband – a fast and powerful channel by which to connect your computer to the Internet.

CBL – computer-based learning. Learning that uses computers. This was a forerunner of e-learning.

CD-ROM learning – learning from a Compact Disc Read Only Memory, which has a high storage capacity.

Conference boards or **discusssion rooms** (asynchronous) – for example *FirstClass* or within a VLE. Places where discussions can be held by threads or themes. People can respond in their own time to questions / comments posted by others.

Email attachments – electronic files attached to email messages.

Emailing – sending messages electonically via a computer. This can be used for communicating one to one or, via mailing lists, to groups of people.

Internet / Net – networks of computers linked together around the world.

Intranet – an internal network within an institutuion / organisation / company.

LANs – Local Area Networks, many are available at no charge, such as in airports, railway stations – and Starbucks!

M-learning – Learning via mobile technology.

Modem – a device by which a computer is connected to the telephone line.

One to one (or more) **chat** (synchronous) – for example, *Netmeeting, ichat.* Conversations take place in real time by being online at the same time as one or more other people.

Online learning – learning by going 'online', that is, by connecting to information on the Internet, often via a telephone line.

Server – a powerful computer that is used to store collections of web pages that can be accessed via the Internet.

Service Provider – an organisation or company that hosts a server and provides both access to web pages via the Internet and launches web pages to the Internet on behalf of its staff / clients.

URL – Uniform Resource Locator or address of a website – usually beginning with 'http://'.

Virtual learning environment (VLE) – a powerful computer that is used to provide students with access to a variety of electronic learning resources in-house. The terms 'electronic learning environment' (ELE) and 'managed learning environment' (MLE) are also used.

Web-based learning – learning using web pages.

Web browser – software used to access websites, for example, *Internet Explorer* and *Netscape.*

Web page – an electronic 'page' on which information is held and displayed on-screen.

Website – a collection of related web pages.

World Wide Web (commonly abbreviated to **WWW** or simply the **web**) – the vast collection of information available around the world on web pages.

Figure 3.1   Glossary of terms used in e-learning

3.4 Online learning

An increasing number of course leaders are providing information and learning materials online, in the form of course websites. Access to these is likely to be restricted and you will need a user-name and password from your course leader to use them. These sites will typically have some or all of the following information / features:

- Programme and module information
- Learning outcomes for each unit of study
- Assessment details, including dates for submission of assignments
- Schedule of learning
- Interactive learning materials
- Opportunities for self-assessment questions (SAQs) and feedback (see Section 3.8 below)
- University / college staff information and contact details
- Links to lots of other resources, both internal and external to your college / university, including electronic library resources (see Chapter 6 for more details)

Some of the above may be an additional version of information provided in paper-based format, but some elements may well be available in the online version only. In some instances e-learning will be used to *supplement* traditional forms of face to face learning or paper-based distance learning, in other cases e-learning *replaces* other forms of learning. In many ways electronic learning uses the same methods of learning as traditional forms of learning; it is the tools that are used that are very different. The key difference about e-learning is that you, the student, have far more control over the resources that can be accessed and the order in which those materials are used. This is generally a positive thing, but it can also lead to feelings of being lost out there in cyberspace and in need of some form of guidance. This guidance is provided on the course website by your module tutor, particularly through the use of navigation aids.

Increasingly though the responsibility for learning is being shifted towards the learner *learning*, rather than the teacher *teaching*. Online learning is playing a significant part in this shift and many learners are now expected to work with others online to learn collaboratively via discussion rooms. (See later in this chapter and Section 7.1 for more information.)

3.5 Email and mailing lists

Email is perhaps the most common form of e-learning used. It provides a very fast and relatively cheap way in which students can receive support and information both from their tutors and from other students on their course – their peers. It is the electronic equivalent of calling in to see your tutor in their office or chatting to a fellow student before, after or even during class. In order to use email you will need, as well as having the necessary hardware and software, to register with an email provider, many of whom provide their service at no charge. Emails can usually be downloaded from the service provider very quickly at the cost (to you) of a short local phonecall. In some countries local calls are provided at no charge by the telephone companies. Many people can also access their email by going to the website maintained by the service provider. This means that emails can be accessed from any networked computer around the world – very convenient if you are travelling as part of your job. (See also guidance on emailing in Section 7.1 on Working with others.)

Mailing lists can be used to share information via email with people who have a common interest. An electronic mailing list is quite similar to a postal mailing list in that it is a method of distributing the same information to lots of different people. Mailing lists are typically used to discuss work with colleagues / students at other institutions, share news, collaborate on projects and publications, announce jobs and conferences, and keep in touch with current developments in your subject area. In order to get information from a mailing list you need to subscribe – that is, you need to ask that your name and email address be added to the list. Other people can then send information to you and others on the mailing list simply by posting a message to a single email address. These messages are then forwarded to all members of the list.

There are a number of different services you can use for finding out about what mailing lists exist and how to join them. *JiscMail* hosts a wide number of different mailing lists for the academic community in the UK. You can search their website (http://www.jiscmail.ac.uk) for mailing lists on a subject of interest to you, but you will need to keep your search term fairly broad, for example, 'literature', rather than 'Dickens'. You will find instructions for joining and leaving lists. There is also a link from their website to lots of other directories of lists.

3.6 Virtual learning environments (VLEs)

There are now several commercially available VLEs: *WebCT* and *Blackboard* are just two examples. Some universities, including the University of Leeds, have developed their own in-house virtual learning environments. Put simply, VLEs are electronic equivalents of the resources available in real university or college buildings. You are likely to be asked to access information and / or study materials and to contribute to discussions within one. Most VLEs can be accessed from anywhere in the world via the Internet, using a web browser such as *Netscape* or *Internet Explorer*.

Most VLEs, including *WebCT* and *Blackboard*, have the following facilities:

- Access to web-based learning materials
- Structured gateways to other internal and external electronic resources
- Discussion rooms of defined membership
- Self-assessment multiple-choice questions with feedback
- Short answer tests
- Secure delivery of essay material
- Satisfaction questionnaires

You will need a username and password to access specific materials for your course. As a registered student at your institution you may well have already received information on how to obtain your username and password for this resource.

3.7 Discussion rooms / conference boards / bulletin boards

These are a useful way of holding discussions with tutors and other students when regular face to face tutorials or seminars are not feasible.

There are facilities for some form of electronic discussion within all of the electronic learning environments mentioned above. They provide a variety of synchronous and asynchronous systems. In addition, *FirstClass* is a conferencing system used by some course providers. It integrates electronic mail with group conferencing in a graphical bulletin board style. It also supports synchronous real time 'chat' with other users.

Electronic discussions can provide a very valuable and stimulating forum for intellectual debate. Sometimes a large cohort of students on one course is sub-divided into groups of six or eight students / learners / participants who cooperate electronically in some form of group task. Some tutors provide two types of electronic rooms for a particular cohort of students – one for the academic work and a second one for more informal chat. The tutor is likely to act as a moderator of the discussion in the academic room, but may not necessarily intervene or make any contribution to the discussion. In some cases the tutors do not have access to the second, informal room, and these rooms become very much the electronic equivalent of the common room or bar (students have to provide their own beverages!). However, the university or college will reserve the right to monitor all electronic communication to ensure that the regulations are not being broken. You are likely to find some sort of conditions for use of computer systems in your student handbook.

All systems use some form of threading for particular themes in the discussion so that users and moderators can keep track of different elements or themes that arise. Many systems enable tutors and students to upload documents, for example *Word* or *PowerPoint* files, that are appropriate to share with other members of the group. It is possible to read the contributions of others to such a discussion without actually making a contribution yourself – commonly known as being a 'lurker' (but also as a browser or vicarious learner / participant). However, the manager or moderator of a group (and sometimes all members of the group) will be able to see who has been reading the messages but not contributing.

Sometimes an element of your course may be assessed by your contribution to a discussion room. If this is the case at some stage in your course, you need to check what the criteria for assessment are and ensure that you meet them. It is not usually simply a case of making a contribution, but rather you are assessed by the quality of that contribution. In some higher level courses everyone in the group may be provided with questions for discussion that are based on readings that you have been given earlier. Your contribution may well be judged, not just on what you post to the discussion room, but on how effective you are in prompting contributions from others. (See also guidance on group discussions in Section 7.1 on Working with others.)

3.8 Self-assessment questions (SAQs)

SAQs referred to in Section 2.4 are often provided by electronic means. They may be found either within the VLE (for example *Blackboard)* or on a web page linked from within the VLE or from another website provided for your course. They can also be made available on a CD-ROM, so that you don't have to work online.

Online assessments are quick and easy to complete and they provide you with virtually instant feedback about your progress. They are not intended primarily to judge you, but rather to provide you with the opportunity to recognise where more help or work is needed and with ideas for appropriate further study.

3.9 Streaming video, such as *Boxmind* or *Click and Go*

Some module materials include an element of online video, for example a few minutes of a pre-recorded video clip accessed from within the module website. Such materials may have been created using the *Boxmind* or *Click and Go* technology. This allows you to see video with sound and accompanying text of the sound script on screen at the same time. Some materials also include additional *PowerPoint* slides, such as might be used during a face to face lecture. In order to access these materials your computer needs to be equipped with the appropriate additional hardware and software, that is speakers, video and sound cards, and some form of media player. Such learning materials are still relatively rare; if your module does include them your module leader should give you detailed information on how to set up your computer.

3.10 Video / teleconferencing

Technology also exists that enables digital broadcasting and receipt of video / television. Some programmes of study include an element of this in the form of a lecturer at an institution giving a live lecture to students at various remote computer clusters or individual PCs around the world. Such technology is currently used more often to bring a lecturer, remote from an institution, to students on campus, since the equipment needed is still extremely expensive. However, the increasing use of digital 'monitor-top' camcorders by individuals makes the use of this method of delivery more likely in the not very distant future.

Activity Nine

Although you are unlikely to encounter all of the above elements of e-learning on your course, you will probably be expected to use one or two of them. If you have already received the course documentation use this to make a list of e-learning methods due to be used on each of your modules and, if possible, try to familiarise yourself with them at this stage.

If you already have the necessary hardware and software to access the Internet, go to your course website and explore. There may be a link from that website into the VLE that you will be using.

3.11 Viruses and backing up work

With increased access to electronic resources comes the increased risk of receiving a computer virus, especially if you are downloading files from other people. Some of these can be devastating, destroying your work in seconds. Other less serious ones can still be really annoying and difficult to eliminate.

The first thing is to ensure that you have anti-virus software on the computer(s) you are using – at home, work or the study centre. The software will warn you if you do receive a virus and give instructions on how to deal with it. You need to regularly update the software.

Second, and important for many reasons, not just with regard to viruses, is to keep a backup of all of your work. Hours of work can be lost in seconds if something goes wrong with your software and your computer 'hangs' on you. Experts might be able to help you retrieve lost data files, but most of us don't have such sophisticated skills – best to use a set of floppy discs a zip disc, or a writable CD-ROM to make copies of all your files at very frequent intervals.

> 'A computer with Internet [connection] or access to one easily IS VITAL. It will become your best friend and your worst enemy. Keep backup discs of all work. This sounds so obvious and yet several people lost whole assignments and I 'lost' 3 transcripts which took me 3 further days to re transcribe.'

Summary of Chapter 3

> In this chapter you have:
>
> * Considered the various types of e-learning that you are likely to encounter whilst registered as a student
> * Had the opportunity to familiarise yourself with some of the e-methods you will need to use on your course
> * Had the opportunity to explore your course website and possibly your VLE

4 Practicalities of studying

Introduction

This chapter deals with the *where*, the *when* and the *how* of your studying. As you read through each of the following elements, make notes (as suggested below) of the conclusions you come to about *yourself.*

4.1 Place of study

> 'Having two children and demands from the household I found that studying at home was a frustrating experience with constant inter-ruption, unless it could be done early in the morning or late in the evening. The solution for me is simply to block out all day Saturday and go to my office to study and don't leave until the study I want to accomplish is completed . . . also during the week, sometimes I will stay late at work . . . to complete the assignments.'

Finding the right place (and time) to study is crucial and preferences vary with the individual. Some people can pick up their materials anywhere (on the train or bus, in a busy staff room, in the lounge) and instantly start to concentrate. Most people, however, need a special space for study – one where, when you sit down, you immediately move into study mode and where you are not distracted. Apart from anything else, it is helpful if you can leave your books undisturbed from one period of study to the next and you are then ready to start again straight away, rather than spending the first 15 minutes sorting out where you were up to last time. The choice of working with or without music in the background is obviously yours, but there are some simple pointers to what will aid concentration and promote good health:

- A warm, comfortable room (or part of a room)
- A working area with a good supply of natural light
- A desk / table at a height within the range 66–73 cm
- A comfortable (preferably swivel) chair at the right height for the table
- A computer screen (if using a PC) to which you drop your eyes (rather than straining your neck to look up to it) and which is ideally 50 cm in front of you and at a right angle to the window
- Room to spread out the books currently in use
- Room to store the materials not currently in use in an organised way, such as in labelled ring-binders or files
- An answerphone so that you are not distracted when studying
- Set times of day for reading and answering emails
- A boring view from the window, so that you don't spend your time watching the world go by!

Difficulty: 'Identifying a study place outside the home [so] that as soon as I entered my mind was in a set to study.'

Strategy: 'I booked a room in a university library for lengths of time.'

Activity Ten

Make a note of the ideal place available to *you* to study. If such a place does not yet exist note down any things you may need to do to find / create somewhere approaching your ideal.

Note your response

4.2 Getting organised

As well as sorting out where you are going to study, there are various other things to plan in advance. Things that you take for granted when you are a full-time student on campus are not always available at your local shop. A supply of stationery items that you may not have bought for a while, such as file paper and loose leaf binders, a hole punch and a stapler, might come in handy. Post-it notes are invaluable and you may want to buy index cards for noting details of references. A wall planner may help with time management, and a highlighter pen may prove an invaluable tool when reading through your learning materials and photocopied articles.

You may have received a booklist when you registered for the course. You might need to order some of these in advance, especially if you don't have a local bookshop or library with a large stock. It can easily take six weeks for a new book to arrive. You may find it quicker or more convenient to buy a book using one of an increasing number of online bookshops available on the web (see Section 6.4 for details).

Activity Eleven

Make a shopping / borrowing list. Don't forget to include a new dictionary if you haven't bought one in recent years. It is crucial that you look up words you haven't encountered before. This will improve your understanding of the course materials and increase your vocabulary.

Note your response

4.3 Pace of study

'Timing is everything. Make sure that you are aware of submission dates and do what it takes to meet them. The pressure of the course mounts up considerably if work is rushed and late. You have to feel that you are in control of the course. Extensions for one module just leave less time for the next.'

The pace of study might be imposed on you by the course tutor, in so far as particular assignments are due in on specific days, or you have to prepare for a group seminar by a certain date. Alternatively, you may be able to choose your own pace at which to work through the programme of study. Either way you need to plan your study time (see Section 4.6 Time management). Some people do very little for weeks, then cram towards the end of a module, others work more evenly throughout the module. Clearly the second is the safer option. Either way, effective study requires a significant amount of time.

Activity Twelve

Make a note of *your* intended study pattern – just your general approach, not the detail at this stage.

> *Note your response*

'I found writing [the] title of [an] assignment and [the] objectives and submitting these by a deadline prior to commencing written work extremely valuable in that: i) you had to really focus your thoughts and get on with the literature search instead of leaving things to the last minute; and ii) once agreed with supervisor it prevented me from changing my mind.'

'You . . . need to identify topics and start literature searching early so that you can get the information and complete the assignment.'

4.4 Time of study

'It is important to set aside time every day, or nearly every day for study. A lot of little bits spread over a week is much better than the whole day every Saturday.'

Whether the pace of study is decided by you or imposed externally, you still have the choice about when you study – morning, afternoon or night. Some people are able to set aside full days or half days in which to study, others manage with evenings or snatched hours here and there. For some it is their choice, for others it is a case of using whatever time is available, when it is available. Ideally you should build into your week specific times in good-sized chunks when you intend to work, and stick to them.

'Block out certain days for study only.'

'Get into a routine.'

'Allocate time specifically at the same time each week for (a) allocated reading time (b) allocated writing time.'

As the above comments from students show, there is no *right* way for everyone – you have to discover what suits you.

Activity Thirteen

Make a quick note of those days of the week / times of the day when you think you are regularly going to be able to study. (You will be asked to look at this issue in more detail in Activity Seventeen.)

Note your response

4.5 Periods of study

Most of us benefit from short frequent breaks in the course of our studies: every 30 to 40 minutes seems to be the norm. Pushing yourself beyond this can lead to concentration lapsing and recall of what you have studied being much reduced. You don't have to have a cup of coffee *every* time of course: a bit of a stretch or a very short walk would be just as effective and much healthier! Others find that a fairly long period of study followed by a long break suits them best. Only you can decide which suits you. Once you have decided honestly which suits you, try and stick to this and take breaks at the right time for the right reasons.

Activity Fourteen

Make a note of the period of study that you know or think will suit you best.

Note your response

If you are using a computer for a lot of your study activities it is advisable to take frequent short breaks rather than less frequent longer breaks. This helps prevent headaches, eyestrain and aches and pains in the hands, wrists, arms, neck, shoulders and back. Either formally build in other study activities at regular intervals or take informal breaks to have a stretch of your arms and legs.

4.6 Time management

'I consider the most important aspect to be time management, whether in finding time to do the work or in keeping up with the studies at an even rate of progress. All other considerations pale into insignificance and tend to fall into place if you can manage the time.'

Having considered each of the issues in Sections 4.3 to 4.5 above, you are now in a strong position to get down to some serious consideration of how you are going to manage your time. Managing your time effectively and efficiently is one of the most difficult things to achieve – you need to become expert at *creating* time. At the beginning of your studies the months may seem to stretch endlessly ahead of you but unless you make a plan and work to it you will find that time goes by very fast.

Activity Fifteen

Take a few minutes now to reflect upon *your* attitude towards time and on how well you use time. Note down a sentence or two that encapsulates these thoughts.

Note your response

'Whilst time management would seem to be a good plan, I found I had to be 'in the mood'. However when I was I didn't want to take a break if things were going well (i.e. absorbing written material or working on assignments).'

'The conflicting demands of studying, work and home life must be known to all. It is far harder than being a full-time student on campus and in my mind should always be recognised as such.'

Commentary

Some people know that they are well organised and use their time effectively every day. Others will acknowledge that they are 'hopeless' at planning the use of their time – things 'just happen' and they react as best they can, as soon as they can. Most of us are somewhere between these two points.

Even when we try to discipline our use of time, other factors such as physical or mental tiredness or illness (our own or that of a member of our family) may come into play and we are thrown off course. This is inevitable and we need to build in a degree of flexibility into any plan of study that we make. If we get too anxious about not being on schedule, that anxiety will be counter-productive. Our minds need to be capable of concentration and creativity. You are likely to need to modify your plan as the work progresses. Indeed a key component of time management is regularly reviewing and amending schedules.

Most people would welcome the opportunity to have long periods of time to devote to their studies but that is a luxury enjoyed by the few. Whilst it can be quite difficult to switch to study-related activities from doing other things, that is often the reality. Some people can combine the two, such as having ideas about your studies whilst doing household tasks or taking physical exercise. However, it is important to sometimes have a complete break from studying as well. You will be more productive if you're feeling mentally and physically refreshed. Digging in the garden for an hour or going for a brisk walk can work wonders.

'I found one of the problems . . . was reduced concentration after a busy working day. The coping strategies which I employed were, to take exercise (to clear my head!), to have a break if ideas were not forthcoming and finally allowing myself *not* to study if I was over tired.'

There are many aspects to time management, but there are two aspects that we need to look at in detail here. The first is planning, as far as possible, the whole period of your study (one semester or one, two or three years or more?), dividing the years / semesters into parts (months?) and setting a timetable for yourself. The second is looking at a typical week within this period of time, and working out how you are to find a specified number of hours per week in which to study.

Study schedule

Taking the above commentary and your own inclinations into account, you need to draw up a realistic schedule for the whole of your study period. Remember that you need to allow plenty of time for seminar preparation (if these are included) and for completing your assignments. The deadline for these will usually be imposed by external factors, such as the submission date of your assignment or a schedule for seminars – these should be stated in the student handbook. (You might, at a later stage, have to build in dates agreed with a group of your fellow students for informal support groups as well.) Using these dates you can calculate how many months / weeks you have between now and your deadlines and design a study schedule. This might simply be a list of tasks with proposed completion dates against them, but in order to see the relationship between different tasks it is better to draw up some form of table or chart which is divided up into monthly, weekly or even daily sections on one axis and by a series of tasks on the other (this is known as a Gantt chart).

Figure 4.1 Course study schedule

Year:Month	1:1	1:2	1:3	1:4	1:5	1:6	1:7	1:8	1:9	1:10	1:11	1:12	2:1	2:2	2:3	2:4	2:5	2:6	2:7	2:8	2:9	2:10	2:11	2:12
Introductory reading	↑	↑	↑																					
Residential			↑																					
Module 1				↑	↑	↑																		
Assignment 1						↑	↑																	
Module 2								↑	↑	↑														
Assignment 2										↑	↑													
Module 3												↑	↑	↑										
Assignment 3														↑	↑									
Module 4																↑	↑	↑						
Assignment 4																		↑	↑					
Dissertation																↑	↑	↑	↑	↑	↑	↑		
Revision for finals																						↑	↑	↑
Final written examinations																								↑

Strategy: 'Planning a timetable for study and stick[ing] to it – easier said than done.'

'Put built in emergency time near to [the] assignment date – there are always untoward situations which disrupt plans.'

One example of what a study schedule might look like is given in Figure 4.1. This example is of a typical UK two-year part-time masters programme schedule but, of course, you can adapt it to the particular programme and time schedule you are working with. You will see that it includes several months for writing a research dissertation. In fact the planning of your research project (where one is included in your course) and the literature search and preparatory reading for it should ideally start as soon as possible after the start of your course, and certainly no later than the start of the second year of a two-year part-time course. Once you have decided on your research topic, you will need to devise a more detailed study schedule specifically for your research project. Suggestions for what to include in that more detailed schedule, and a great deal more information about doing your research project, are provided in Chapter 8.

Activity Sixteen

Now create a first draft of your own study schedule. You might want to add specific months or weeks (that is, dates) to your schedule or you may simply use the consecutive numbering as in the example in Figure 4.1. Although you will not be able to fill in the tasks in detail until you have finished working through this guide and perhaps received more information from your course tutor or fellow students, make a start on drafting your schedule now. You could even include the study of this guide as one of the tasks. You could also make an entry for talking to other students about how they are feeling about starting to study in this way, or a few months on, how they are coping. You could certainly include time for reading any recommended introductory texts and, of course, time for actually working through the learning materials.

Clearly many of the tasks will overlap and will therefore appear in the same week or month of the schedule. Some tasks will have to be completed consecutively rather than concurrently, since you won't be able to start one until you have completed the other. Following up relevant readings for each module, including time for reflection on what you have read, needs to be scheduled before beginning to write the assignments. You also need to build in some allowance for unexpected circumstances that slow you down.

Don't forget to allow for holidays (yours and other people's) and for any significant Holy days and national holidays when people you wish to contact may not be available or facilities you might wish to use may not be accessible.

'Leave time for things to go wrong. Books may not be available, the computer might not work, a family problem may occur.'

Commentary

You need to be flexible within broad limits that are fixed externally (such as the dates for a tutor-marked assignment or the final examination) and regularly review your progress and amend your timetable. Once you start to add a lot of detail, you might be better buying a large, wall year planner so that you can fit everything in.

Remember don't let this activity / process become a substitute for real work!

Weekly planner

Although some weeks will vary from others (especially if your work involves different shifts in different weeks) most of us have some sort of pattern to each week. It is usually possible, therefore, to build in study time at the same time or times each week. If you are on a mixed-mode course of study you will, of course, have certain fixed times

Hour of the day	Monday	Tuesday	Wednesday	Thursday	Friday	Saturday	Sunday

Figure 4.2 Weekly planner

Note: Since people begin and end their days at different times no details have been included in the Hour boxes. A 16-hour day has been assumed, but if you sleep for considerably more or less than 8 hours you could always add or delete rows / hours accordingly in your own version of this planner. Half-hours could be created by dividing the boxes.

when you need to attend your college or university for the face to face sessions.

'No such thing as balancing time demands, some weeks do more of one [activity] than [an]other.'

Activity Seventeen

You will probably find it helpful to sketch out a grid as in Figure 4.2 showing a typical week in your life, including first the things that you *have* to do each week, then those regular commitments that you would prefer not to have to drop whilst you are studying. Then try to add in time for studying in those places where you have free time. Sometimes it will be useful to have an extended period in which to study, but you could also make use of other shorter periods of time for doing a fairly short activity or going to the library on a regular basis, if one is within easy reach, to keep up-to-date by reading a journal in your subject area, for example. (Increasingly journals are available online, so you may not need to physically go to the library.)

In practice you may find your weeks turn out to be far from typical and you need to be flexible in the number of hours you spend each week on your study. Sometimes study activity will be more intensive than others, especially as a deadline for an assignment approaches.

'I have found it best to plan to spend half to one hour a night regularly, with extra when possible. Most people can find half an hour during the day / evening, even when the kids are screaming. It is absolutely essential to be disciplined about spending the time, and spreading [it] out in this way makes it much easier to keep up. For commuters like myself, the time on the train / bus / tube can be very usefully spent – instead of reading the paper or the latest novel or sleeping!! If it's too chaotic at home, stay at work for an extra half hour. Spending regular time is probably the most important thing you can do.'

Commentary

It has to be said that what happens in reality often bears little resemblance to the neat timetable you have created. Many people have to learn to do more than one thing at a time. But when it comes to studying, most of us need to give it our undivided attention if we are going to do it well.

Clearly, if it looks as though you are not going to find enough time to study within your current lifestyle, something has got to change. It may be that you need to delegate more of your work tasks to colleagues, or domestic tasks to other members of your family (assuming that they are willing to take on more responsibility!). Or it may be a question of having to prioritise your tasks and ensure that those at the top of the list (that you really *have* to do) are definitely done at the beginning of the day or week, with the less essential ones dropping off the bottom of the list if necessary. Sometimes it may be necessary to make more radical changes if you are going to find time for study. A favourite pastime might have to be given up for a while, or you may have to re-negotiate your working hours temporarily if there is no other way to find the time. (If you are completing your course to improve your skills in the workplace, your employer might be more sympathetic to this idea.) Whatever you decide to do, you have to be sure that this is the right thing and be firm in your efforts to find the necessary time to devote to your studies.

A useful aspect of the whole process is to reflect from time to time upon the plan that you made and compare what you actually did with what you had planned to do. This review can then be used to inform a revised plan, building in more realistic time allocations for different activities. Don't worry about having to change your plans sometimes – the important part of the whole activity is to help you to think strategically.

Keeping the balance

If you are following a mixed-mode course that includes some modules by distance learning alongside other modules by traditional face to face methods you will need to take care that the distance learning elements don't get squeezed out by the pressure put upon you by your face to face tutors. You may find it helpful to request an occasional face to face tutorial with your distance learning module tutors (if they are available) even if this isn't actually required as part of your course attendance. You could also try to arrange an informal get together from time to time with your fellow distance learning students. These two strategies can help keep alive the reality of your distance learning modules and serve as a reminder of the work that needs to be done for them.

> 'Time: huge factor, not to be underestimated. To keep on a full time job and study is very stressful. Hobbies and social life will have to be put on hold.'

4.7 How will you use your time?

It's all very well having decided exactly when you are going to have your times for study, but the really important part is using that time in the most effective way. Once you have decided when you are going to study in a particular week you will find it useful to set yourself specific tasks for that week. If an assignment is due at the beginning of the following week there is little room for negotiation, but you could still set times for specific aspects of preparing for and writing up that assignment, such as: read Chapter 3 of . . . and make notes; write the first draft; edit the first draft; complete the bibliography; and so on. Don't forget to leave time for thinking and reflection too.

> 'Sometimes the task, e.g. [an] essay seemed overwhelming therefore [it was] better to break down [the] task [in]to small achievable outcomes within . . . small study slots.'

If an assignment is not imminent it is all too easy to relax and think that you have all the time in the world for your studying, but it's amazing how quickly the weeks fly by. By setting yourself goals for each week / day or even by the hour (and meeting them!) you give your studying purpose and meaning and you will get a sense of achievement on completion of each task that will feed your motivation. It is important to distinguish between those tasks that are essential, those that are desirable, and those that are neither but are nevertheless worthwhile.

You need to be quite self-disciplined in this whole process, not just when it comes to starting on a particular task, but knowing when to stop as well. It is easy to stretch out a task you are thoroughly enjoying for several hours, knowing that you have a more difficult one to start next. In other words, you have to manage tasks as well as time. Sometimes you also have to accept that the work you produce is *good enough* for the purpose, even though it is not the *best* that you could have achieved given unlimited time and energy.

> 'Time planning is the most important aspect. Not to say 'I've got a free day' and sit down after breakfast to plough through it till you drop. Be realistic. Set a study period of say 2 hours which will include a plan of what you hope to achieve in that time.'

There may be times when you genuinely need to revise your plans – studying is quite an unpredictable activity – but a regular review of what you plan and what you actually achieve is likely to be quite revealing. The occasional amendment is to be expected – but under-achievement of set goals every week may be cause for concern.

Summary of Chapter 4

> In this chapter you have:
>
> *   Considered various study patterns that people use
> *   Made decisions about where and when you would prefer to study
> *   Prepared a draft study schedule for the whole course
> *   Sketched out a plan of your weekly study pattern

5   Getting support

Introduction

You may feel that you are quite happy to get on with your studying totally on your own and don't need any support or input from anyone. Some people do manage to be fully independent learners for the duration of their course and simply turn up at the set time to take a formal examination and pass with flying colours. However, these are certainly the exception. Most of us (and I speak from the experience of being a distance learner as well as a tutor of distance learners) need support from someone at some stage in our studies.

Feelings of confidence and enthusiasm are likely to be mixed with some feelings of doubt and apprehension when embarking upon any new project, and starting a distance learning course is likely to create a similar mix too. If in the course of your studies the negative feelings begin to dominate, however, it is important to do something about it, as they could reduce your self-confidence and lead to a downward spiralling in your studies. That's when you need to know who to turn to for support. Talking about your feelings will help to give you some sort of perspective about them and hopefully provide ideas for overcoming the problems leading to the negativity. Try to remind yourself that this period of studying will not last forever. Try too to build in some time for rest and relaxation alongside your working and studying life.

'My leisure time was reduced whilst distance learning but I accepted this, as it was only for a comparatively short span of my life.'

5.1 Support from your tutor(s)

'You can't have enough contact with staff – it keeps you sane and on the right track . . . students who are in distance learning need much more contact with tutors etc. than regular University students.'

Keeping in touch with your tutors will provide your link with the people who can speak with authority on any aspect of the academic content of your course. (You may have several tutors if your course consists of several modules.) Although the benefits of getting support from other students are many, it is your tutors who are experts in their fields and who will often (but not always) be the ones who have written the learning materials. It is also your tutors who will interpret your own ideas on all aspects of the course, marking your assignments and ultimately deciding on a grade for your work: it is as well to seek feedback from them at various stages throughout each module rather than leaving it to the formal assessments.

The opportunities provided to contact your tutors will vary from course to course: they may include or exclude particular methods of communication, such as phone or email, and may have a time limit imposed. You need to establish at a very early stage what your opportunities are (see Section 9.2). Whatever means of communication are available you need to do some preparation before any substantial contact with tutors (or indeed with anyone else from whom you need help – such as your workplace mentor or, the course administrator). You need to be clear yourself about the points you wish to discuss – you may find it helpful to write them down beforehand. This will help to ensure that neither your time, nor that of your tutor, is wasted.

Your tutor is the key person to provide information about new resources available in a specific subject field (journal articles, websites, and so on). S/he is also best placed to give their views on new developments in the field or to help you discover your views on certain issues. This will help you develop your own ideas further. The feedback you receive from your tutors to your formal and informal assessments is crucial. Assessment is not just about a process of making judgements and allocating grades: it is another opportunity to learn, if you carefully consider the feedback provided.

5.2 Support from other students

Some course tutors organise formal learning groups or sets for their students' mutual support, but even where this is not the case, you will find it is well worth the effort to set up something on an informal basis.

> 'Peer support was the greatest asset.'
>
> '. . . the key issue . . . is the lack of contact with both students and tutors / lecturers. Of course e-mail is a great invention, and it helps. But there's no substitute for actually meeting other people and discussing things generally – whether it's course related or simply the price of coffee in Starbucks.'

The benefits of being in touch with other students are several. The benefits of meeting together face to face if at all possible will usually outweigh the difficulties of making all of the arrangements to be away from home for a couple of days for a short residential session and the hassle and cost of the travelling. However, you can still be supported by and support other students whom you will never meet face to face.

> '. . . a . . . programme via distance learning draws people together through adversity. Fellow students are a strong support.'

Why do you need other students?

> Strategy: 'Being able to talk through issues, concerns, ideas with another student on a regular basis.'

Others can help you to learn

As referred to in Section 2.6 talking things through with others can constitute the 'apply' part of the learning cycle. Having to express the ideas that have been swimming around in your own head for some time is an excellent way of refining those ideas, especially when others are prepared to listen carefully and give constructive feedback. It also provides the opportunity for you to become familiar with using academic language specific to your course or subject discipline.

It is still generally regarded in most cultures that the academic tutor is *the* expert in his or her field. It is, however, becoming increasingly accepted that they are not necessarily the sole authority on a subject, and that fellow students or peers on a course can also make a significant contribution to the construction of knowledge. This is especially true where the students involved have a wide and varied experience of the workplace and of life in general.

> 'At times there were feelings of isolation and lack of contact with others. This is when a list of willing fellow students' telephone numbers and emails can be so helpful. My closest friend was not usually feeling low when I was, and vice versa. The mutual support was invaluable.'

You might have informal discussions or you may agree in advance that all members of the group will read a particular journal article or section of the learning materials that will form the basis of your discussion. Group members may be willing to discuss an assignment topic before you each start to write it, or to read each other's draft assignments before submission.

Others can lift your spirits and boost your confidence

Isolation can be very destructive. The general support that is available from other students on the same course can give a great boost to your flagging morale, especially when you find that others have found a particular unit of the course materials just as difficult as you have. And even if you are the only one not to have grasped a particular concept, you are very likely to learn by listening to others discussing it. Conversely you can help your fellow students by making an input to group discussion.

> 'Study days gave me useful information but also allowed me contact with other students to discuss problems and let off steam.'

Others can motivate you

If you know you have a group meeting scheduled for a couple of weeks' time this may give you the push that you need to get through the next unit of materials. You can then talk things through with others with the same study interests as yourself before you have to express your own ideas on paper in the form of a written assignment for your tutor. Enthusiasm is infectious.

> 'I befriended a fellow student and we supported each other over the telephone. We both had times of self doubt, but negative thoughts were soon dispersed, as we listened to each other's concerns and offered encouragement to one another.'

Meeting others can be fun

Making friends with others on your course can be one of the most rewarding aspects of studying. Meeting others can be an important social occasion as well as an intellectual one.

How can you keep in touch?

> 'It is of course possible to contact other students – but it is not like having informal discussion with a larger group round coffee etc.'

Since communication with others in a group is more effective if you can actually meet face to face, organising an informal study group in your geographical area, even if one isn't organised officially by your university or college, is likely to prove very worthwhile. Several courses have an occasional face to face meeting, often at the start of each module; it is then much easier to contact others subsequently by various other means. Where students on your course are so dispersed that it just isn't possible to meet, try to exchange phone numbers or email addresses, or ask the course tutor to organise telephone conferencing, computer conferencing, or an electronic discussion group via the course website. Very often someone poses a question via such a forum that you really wanted to ask, but didn't like to, for fear of appearing ignorant. Remember that we can only learn what we acknowledge that we don't already know.

> 'One of the most useful things I have found is developing a group of friends on the same course, with whom you can share problems. With most people being on email at home or work this is very easy.'

5.3 Support from the course administrator

> '. . . the Administrator was indefatigable in advising, answering queries, seeing we got material, putting us in touch with . . . and other personnel.'

Your first point of contact with your college or university is probably with the course administrator for the course on which you enrol (they may be called something other than this, such as course secretary or admissions officer). S/he will very likely be able to deal with most of your queries about the course: dates of attendance at the institution for short courses, submission dates for assignments, format in which assignments must be submitted, how you can contact your tutors or other students, and so on.

A friendly face (or voice) can make all the difference when you're feeling as if you don't belong or are a bit swamped with the many aspects of your studies with which you have to cope. A quick email or short phone call will usually be enough to get things sorted. Details of who to contact and how and when to contact them should be included in the course handbook. (The friendly face of one particular course administrator at the University of Leeds was mentioned more than once in the comments collected from students for this guide.)

5.4 Support from family and friends

> 'I feel it is important to enlist the help and co-operation of other family members and friends.'
>
> 'Good family support was available to me and without this I don't think I would have coped.'

Included in the comments received from students are many that emphasise the importance of support from those closest to you. It may be tempting to try to keep everything to do with studying totally separate from the rest of your life, but (as was mentioned earlier) your studying will affect and place demands on others. The wise student is the one who cultivates mutual understanding about their studies with those with whom they live and socialise. If you are fortunate enough to have people who take an interest in what you are doing, don't shut them out. They may not be able to empathise with you at a subject-specific level but they will be able to give emotional and practical support. That said, you also need to ensure that they know when you want to be left alone to study. But having someone cook you an evening meal at the end of a full day at work followed by a couple of hours study is wonderful!

> 'Be amazingly organised. Sit the family down and realistically look at the essential household jobs, who is going to do them and when. Be realistic, they may not get done as you would do them, but they will get done. Little and often. Obtain all the local take away menus, and buy iron free clothes. I paid my older children to Hoover, empty the dishwasher, use the washing machine, and make the tea. I was broke, but these things did get done.'

5.5 Support from those at work

This may be of a formal nature through some form of mentoring scheme or it may simply be a colleague or line manager taking a helpful interest in what you are doing. A growing number of organisations in the UK and elsewhere operate a system of workplace mentors who are responsible for supporting the development of one or more colleagues. If you already have such a mentor they may regard supporting you in your studies as an extension of this role. Such a role will complement that of your academic tutor. S/he will help you make connections between your academic course and your workplace.

'Mentorship was new to me, but as a distance learner I identified a senior [colleague] in my organisation [who] provided a mentor role throughout the study. This added support from a different angle, and was constructive in enabling correct action to be taken in times of stress. It also helped me to identify the key people to speak to regarding work based difficulties and study, and was supportive in negotiating for time to undertake the research part of the [Degree].'

Whether or not such a scheme exists in your organisation, if your studies are related to your work, the importance of forging a good relationship with those from whom you will need information or cooperation cannot be over-emphasised. They could be crucial in helping you to gain access to information and people within your organisation that are needed to help you complete your assignments. They may also be willing to give comments on your assignments before you hand them to your tutor, give you ideas of topics for discussion or group work, or supervise you whilst you practise skills that you are learning. You may even find that you are entitled to a limited amount of study leave.

'It may be appropriate to suggest that students negotiate more than the set study days off from work for the course. Perhaps applying for funding to enable 'backfill', etc.'

Even if your studies are not directly related to your work it would be as well to talk to your line manager about what you are intending to do before you begin. You may need her / his understanding and support at some stage, such as when you need to take a day's leave in order to meet a looming deadline for an assignment. You need to be clear about whether or not it is acceptable to use IT or photocopying facilities at work for study-related tasks, and if these can be done in working hours or only after the end of the working day.

Strategy: 'Having helpful colleagues.'

Activity Eighteen

Fix up a time to talk to work colleagues and / or your line manager. Make a note of those areas where there was agreement about what assistance / support you might expect.

> *Note your response*

Summary of Chapter 5

In this chapter you have:

- Learned how previous students have benefited from the support of others (tutors, students, work colleagues, family and friends)
- Investigated what support might be available to you during your studies

6 Resources for studying

Introduction

As well as receiving a pack of learning materials from your college or university you will probably receive various lists containing details of supplementary readings, some of which you may need to read before the course starts. You need to make a decision about how many books you need to buy (if any) and find out how many you might be able to borrow. You will also need to search for and retrieve information from many other sources when it comes to preparing for your assignments. It is a good idea to find out now what your sources are, and if necessary to make arrangements in advance for accessing resources.

6.1 Course materials

You will either have already received or will shortly receive a pack of materials related to your course – they may be paper-based, on a CD-ROM or available on the web. If you are following a full programme of study you will probably receive material for each module a couple of weeks before it starts. As well as learning materials you may receive a copy of one or two set textbooks which are integral to your studies, and / or possibly some photocopied articles. Video or audiotapes might also be included for some modules.

> Difficulty: 'Panic when course materials received – new language not work based topics.'
>
> Strategy: 'Start at the back!! Read the references and recommended reading list. Select a recent comprehensive reference which covers the topic in a broad way. Reading this first may give an overview of where the module fits with current practice / application to your work.'

6.2 Library resources

Students are increasingly turning to electronic resources available via the web to find information for completing their assignments. Thousands of electronic journals are now available and these provide far more up-to-date material than books can. If you have access to the web you are likely to go there first when you begin to search for resources. In this sense you are not disadvantaged by being a distance learner. However, many resources are still only available within a conventional (not electronic) library.

> 'Library access is a significant issue. Many books [at my] University [library] which are popular text[s] are [on] one week loan and therefore no use to us as we are . . . 80 miles away.'

A number of different library resources are probably available to you. It is possible (especially if you are employed by a large organisation) that you will find some of the materials you need at work. Even if there is no formal library it is worth asking around various people – you may find the text you need sitting on someone's shelf. Your local public library (where available) may have some of the materials you need, although it is unlikely to have the more specialist journals that you will require. Even if it does not have a lot of the resources you need, it is possible that your local library could provide the quiet, well-lit, warm study space that you need. Some people find that the local branch of their professional association has a small specialist library.

Difficulty: 'Being a long way away from the uni library.'

'When only in [my university] about 1 day per month, getting books out is impossible. I found using a local university library where I live the best option for access any day I want.'

If you do not regularly visit the institution where you are registered, it may be more convenient to visit the library in your local college or university. Many UK university libraries are members of the UK Libraries Plus scheme that allows library access for staff and students of member institutions. Part-time non-distance learning students, and full- and part-time students on distance learning courses, are also allowed borrowing rights. Whichever category you belong to, you will first of all need to obtain a UK Libraries Plus membership card from your own university library, either by visiting one of the library sites or by contacting the distance learning services coordinator or equivalent member of staff in your library. For an up-to-date list of the institutions participating in the UK Libraries Plus scheme, see their website: http://www.uklibrariesplus.ac.uk

If you need to use a library not included in the list, please contact the member of library staff who is responsible for services to distance learners at the university or college where you are a registered student. They may be able to arrange reading or even borrowing rights for you at your local library on an *ad hoc* basis.

Strategy: 'Ensuring that you have access to good library facilities prior to commencing your studies if accessing [your university] is difficult.'

'Visit other university libraries which have related courses and ask if you can join.'

'Local postgraduate library facility [was] very helpful and on [my] doorstep.'

As a registered student at your college or university you are, of course, entitled to use all of its own library facilities. In practice it may not be that easy to do so, especially if you live and work some distance away and never or rarely attend your study institution. If you can attend in person then the usual reference, lending, photocopying and document supply services are obviously available to you.

Various paper library guides may be available to help you with your studies. These could include a guide to services that are available for off-campus users and a guide to referencing bibliographic and electronic resources in your assignments. Ask your course administrator or course leader for copies of these or contact the library direct.

Some specific services may be in place to assist students on distance learning courses, such as:

- Photocopy delivery service for distance learners only
- Postal loan service for distance learners only

Other services that are useful for distance learners may in fact be available for *all* students, for example:

- Off-campus access to electronic library resources
- Telephone renewals
- Online renewals / reservations

> 'Access through the Internet to the university library is wonderful, and apart from physically collecting or returning books you can do almost every other library activity, which is so helpful at distance.'

6.3 Library catalogues

The catalogue of your local academic library is likely to be the starting point in any literature search. In most libraries the catalogue will now be computerised, but in some libraries you may find that the catalogue is still only available on cardboard catalogue cards in drawers. Some may well have a combination of the two systems, where details of the older bookstock have not yet been transferred to the computerised system. Computerised systems vary and you may be advised to seek an introductory leaflet or verbal explanation of how to use it on your first visit to a new library. Usually an online library catalogue will have a subject index, so you can focus a search on a specific subject area. Most also have a keyword search facility, so you can enter your own topic area to get a list of holdings.

You may also have access to the catalogues of other libraries via the computers in your local library or via the Internet using your own PC, for example: the catalogues of other academic libraries, the *British Library* catalogue, or *COPAC* (the catalogue of UK research libraries). Although such catalogues will provide you with bibliographical information, it may take some time to borrow the books themselves via your library's document supply service.

The *British Library Public Catalogue* is available online at: http:// blpc.bl.uk – It is fully searchable and you can order loan items or photocopies direct, either as a registered customer using a customer code and password or as a non-registered customer using a credit card (photocopies only).

6.4 Bookshops

If a book is not easily available from your local library or via the document supply service you may have to consider the option of buying your own copy, especially if you consider it as potentially a key text. You may be fortunate enough to have easy access to a good academic bookshop but even where this is the case, you may find it quicker or more convenient to search for a book yourself using one of an increasing number of online bookshops available on the web. Some such bookshops, for example *Internet Bookshop* (a division of W.H. Smith, http://www.bookshop.co.uk); *Amazon.com* (http:// www.amazon.com); and *Amazon.co.uk* (the UK branch of the US online bookshop, http://www.amazon.co.uk), offer an email notification service of new books which meet your specifications.

You may simply use such services to get bibliographical information on new titles in your subject area or by a particular author with no obligation to buy from them, but if you decide to purchase books from such sources remember that you will probably have to pay postage and package costs on top of the price of the books themselves. (There are other similar 'current awareness services' for books and journals – see Section 8.3 for details.)

You could also try websites that specialise in offering discounted textbooks for sale, for example, *Swotbooks.com*, which offers discounts of up to 40 percent off the full prices. Once you've finished with your textbooks you could even get some money back by selling them through an online service such as *Studentbooks.co.uk*, which puts student buyers and sellers of used books in contact with each other.

6.5 Periodicals / journals in various subject disciplines

Lists of journals, which the library subscribes to, may be available for various subject areas as printed leaflets as well as on the computerised catalogue. Once you (perhaps with the help of your tutor) have identified relevant titles that are held by the library, it is as well regularly to check new issues as they are published for appropriate articles, as there is always a delay before they are included in published abstracts or indexes. It may be possible regularly to receive the Contents pages of the most appropriate journals by email (again see Current awareness services in Section 8.3).

6.6 Abstracts, indexes and electronic databases

Abstracts of and indexes to journal articles may be available in paper or electronic format. Clearly the latter are much quicker to search (see below for more details). Author, title or subject searches will reveal relevant articles. Whilst indexes are useful, an abstract of an article will be a great deal more help in enabling you to decide whether or not to get hold of the full article, since the abstract should give you a clear indication of the contents.

The major abstracting and indexing service for the social sciences is *Web of Science* (a group of databases which includes the *ISI Social Science Citation Index* published by the Institute for Scientific Information). Some material on *Web of Science* is full text, but mostly just a reference and an abstract are given. An extremely useful feature of *Web of Science* is the ability to do a citations search, that is, you can search for articles that make reference to a particular author. This is very useful for finding out who has built on a seminal piece of research. *ABI Global* (part of *ProQuest*), which covers management, marketing and business journals, provides abstracting and indexing services, together with full text articles for recent years from the majority of journals covered. There are several abstracting and index-ing services for scientific literature, for example *INSPEC* (which covers physics, computing and electrical engineering). It should be possible to access all of the above and many more via your study institution's library website.

There are several electronic versions of databases. These mainly contain information about academic journal articles. They may be available in CD-ROM or online format. Many databases include a short summary or abstract for each item to help you assess its value and relevance to your search topic. Most academic libraries will provide access to several different databases, including the *British Newspaper Index* (BNI). Remember that the databases are not in-house catalogues and that you will need to check the library catalogue to find out whether or not the journal or newspaper is held in your library. An increasing number of databases now give access to the electronic version of the articles themselves (see Section 8.3 for more details).

You may well find that some of the journals containing the art-icles which you have selected from abstracts and indexes will not be held in the library where you are doing the searching. In this case you need to be sure of their relevance since you will probably have to pay something towards the cost of each item obtained by the library via the document supply service or you will have the cost and inconveni-ence of having to travel some distance yourself to obtain access to the articles.

Although there are some similarities to searching in various data-bases you will need specific instructions on how to search a particular database. Many libraries will have these instructions both in printed format and available on their web pages. *You will sometimes need to use a registration name and password to gain access to the database*; this will be provided by your library. In some cases they will appear on screen, in others you will need to request them from the library staff. An *Athens* username and password are needed to access several databases. For details of how to obtain your username and password go to your university *Athens* information page.

Off-campus you need to use a personal *Athens* account. This should be generated automatically for all students.

Activity Nineteen

It is probably advisable to make an initial visit at a very early stage to the library that will be your main or sole resource centre. You might do this in person or you may be able to do it just as well by visiting the website of the library to discover what information sources are available.

Make a note of those sources of information likely to be most relevant to your field of study. Some will be printed materials, others CD-ROMs and others will only be available online. It may be that those in the two latter categories can be accessed from your desktop computer without having to go to the library. However, you may need to register at the library in order to be able to access them in this way. Others will only be available using the library's own computers or from a computer on a university or college campus.

If you need to use the electronic resources of the library at the study institution where you are registered, you may need to make arrangements well in advance to receive usernames and passwords electronically or by post to access them, if a personal visit to that library is unrealistic.

6.7 Other electronic resources

In addition to the library's online literature resources, such as databases and e-journals, you may need to search for other websites that contain up-to-date information relevant to your course. Your library may well have compiled a list of quality free websites, selected by specialist subject librarians in consultation with academic staff. Search your library website for details.

Your course tutor or module tutor may also be able to recommend current sites in your particular field. For some of your assignments, though, and certainly for any research project, you will be expected to discover such information for yourself. Various resources are available to help you do this. For information on these and many other electronic resources for studying, see Section 8.3.

6.8 Case studies

Case studies are being used increasingly in higher education to bring to life, in an interesting and relevant way, those ideas and concepts included in your course. They are also forming a growing part of assessment. The degree to which case studies are included on a course clearly will vary according to their relevance to a particular subject area, and within that area from one module to another.

6.9 IT support

It may well be the case that access to a PC with an Internet connection was stated as a prerequisite for your course, in which case you will have had ample time to either purchase your own equipment or arrange access to the necessary equipment at work or elsewhere. Even if it is not stated as a prerequisite, the advantages of having access to such equipment must be clear by now, especially for accessing information, for writing your assignments, and for reducing isolation by being able to communicate electronically with tutors, students and the course administrator.

Computer viruses can be spread very easily through distance learning contacts. Once again let me emphasise the wisdom of installing a proprietary brand virus checker, such as McAfee *VirusScan*, and check all files sent to you before opening them.

Computer services helpdesk

Any help in dealing with problems with your hardware must come from the supplier of that hardware, but you will usually be entitled to support from the Helpdesk at your university or college with any aspect of their networked computer services, including passwords. Whether you are using a PC in a computer cluster or using one at home or work, you should be able to ask for help with accessing electronic sources, provided you are using them via the institution's network. You should be entitled to help with and advice on all of the services that your computer services department supports, as specified in their Service Level Agreement.

Activity Twenty

It would be useful to discover at an early stage what 'Helpdesk' support is available to you. It could take quite a while to find out the specific telephone number you need to ring or email address you need to use for help with a computer network problem. It is much better to have this information already to hand at the time of any mini-crisis in that area.

Summary of Chapter 6

In this chapter you have:

- Investigated what sources of resources are available to you
- Made arrangements (if necessary) to access other resources

7 Making the most of your distance learning experience

Introduction

With limited time and restricted access to resources the distance learner in particular needs to make the most of their learning experience. Whilst it is widely acknowledged that the overall experience of the full-time 18-year-old entering higher education encompasses much more than their learning, the distance learner is often far more focused on the specific task of studying, successfully fulfilling the assessment requirements of the course of study, and obtaining some form of accreditation. That said, most distance learning courses include some element of human contact and it is to be hoped that there is an opportunity for enjoyment and stimulating company (if only in a virtual way) for all of you studying by this mode of delivery.

In this chapter we focus on the detail of the reality of studying, namely:

- Working with others
- Reading
- Note making
- Writing essays (and other prose assignments)
- Revision and exams

Since the book as a whole is intended primarily for those who have previously studied in further or higher education, what follows is a relatively brief guide to those aspects of studying for which you may feel in need of a bit of a refresher. However, there may be some sections that you don't need to work through in detail, especially if you have recently been a student.

7.1 Working with others

The role of the tutor in higher and further education in the UK and elsewhere has changed significantly in recent years. In many instances there has been a shift towards the tutor as a facilitator of learning rather than, or in addition to, a teacher. Although much of your learning as a distance learner will be done by you as an individual, facilitated or helped by materials provided (and probably written) by your tutors and other experts, it is now widely acknowledged that we also have much to learn from our fellow students or peers. The tutor will adopt the role of facilitating that learning between students, but may not necessarily directly involve themselves in the process. In a few instances whole courses are delivered in this manner, but most courses are likely to include some element of group work at some point.

Although working with others on some aspect of your coursework is perhaps more difficult, and certainly different, when studying at a distance, for some courses you may still need to demonstrate that you possess an appropriate set of skills to do so. Learning to work cooperatively and collaboratively with others to complete a project not only benefits you during your time of study but also develops much needed skills for the workplace. When collaborative work is successful it brings benefits to all group participants, since it can reduce the workload of individuals and bring fresh ideas and perspectives to group members. Group working can help you learn more effectively because you will be challenged about your own ideas – thus improving the learning outcomes in Bloom *et al.*'s 'affective' domain (see Section 2.3).

What skills do you need?

Whilst the categories of broad skills needed are essentially the same whether working face to face on campus or at a distance, the methods used to work together will obviously vary and specific skills required differ. In general more effort is required in group work at a distance and it can be slower and more complicated than working alone. Most significantly, the majority of your communication with others may be by technological means, including the use of emails and / or synchronous and asynchronous electronic discussion groups, some of which may be accessed via an electronic learning platform (see Chapter 3 for more details of these methods). You may also be able / expected to use telephone / text messaging or faxing.

The list of skills that you will need to possess to benefit from working with others includes:

- Good communication and interpersonal skills
- Good computer and information technology skills
- Ability to work with others to produce and develop good ideas
- Ability to work with others to achieve outcomes
- Willingness to offer and receive constructive criticism
- Ability to reflect upon your own behaviour in group situations and to be prepared to take steps to change inappropriate or ineffective behaviour

Whilst the principles of good listening and speech skills that are essential for telephone communication can be transferred to the electronic environment, where they equate in some respects with good message writing and message reading, there are specific skills required to communicate effectively electronically and guidelines that need to be followed.

Emailing
- Use a meaningful subject heading in emails.
- Keep your message relatively short. Some people suggest only one screenful, including anything longer in an attached file.
- Include the purpose of the message at the start, then provide more detail thereafter. People can then make a quick judgement about their interest in the message and if it is relevant to them they will not close it before you get to the point.
- It is very difficult to get 'tone of voice' into an email and sometimes the meaning of a message can be misunderstood. Try to check that your message is not going to cause offence. Some people like to use the symbol :-) to reassure the recipient of an email that the message is meant to be friendly. Other people find the practice immensely irritating.

- Read through your email message before posting it and check for ambiguity and spelling mistakes. Although email can be quite ephemeral, many people file their mail into folders for future reference, and meaning can be later misunderstood because of errors.
- Most of us have a limited amount of space in which to store old emails. It is good practice to regularly review messages received; check that you have responded where necessary; delete those no longer required; and archive those that you don't want to delete into appropriately named folders.

Group discussions

- Some of your contributions will be your responses to tasks set by your tutor, others will be reflective responses to what other people have posted.
- Generally your contributions will need to be short and to the point.
- You may want to take some time to think about your contribution and write it out in draft before posting it. It also takes less time connected online to paste in a message previously written in Word, than to type it out there and then on the message board.
- Whilst making it clear to which message you are responding, don't repeat the whole of the previous message in your response.
- When wanting to respond to two different aspects of the same discussion, it is better to post two separate messages.
- Be constructive. Giving critical feedback to other group members is fine if it is accompanied by suggestions of ways to improve their work.
- Sometimes it is more appropriate to email an individual directly to their private email address about something they have posted, rather than to the public discussion forum.
- Beware of hiding behind the anonymity of an electronic discussion group and perhaps including something in a message that you wouldn't say face to face. This is just common courtesy, plus in many courses there will be opportunities for face to face sessions where you will meet up with other group members and therefore have to face those to whom you have mailed messages.

- Everyone needs to take their share of responsibility for making a group discussion work. Try to resist the temptation to only browse or 'lurk' – that is to only read the messages and not participate by making contributions.

Causes of concern, anxiety and frustration

Most of us have concerns or experience some anxiety and frustration when asked to work cooperatively with others.

Activity Twenty-One

Make a list of any concerns, anxieties or frustrations you have experienced in the past or currently have about group work.

> *Note your response*

Commentary

Amongst others, you may have included some of the following:

- You felt that you didn't have much to offer.
- You felt that you could have done the task better on your own.
- Other group members have had too little to offer.
- No one in the group really took the lead or chaired the group and no real progress was made.
- One or two group members dominated the group and didn't listen to the views of others.
- One or two group members did very little work but were awarded equal marks with those who had worked hard.

Group working strategies

How you deal with your anxieties and frustrations will vary enormously from person to person and for the same individual in different situations, but the following might prove helpful:

1   Ask the group tutor to provide guidelines on group work to all participants. They might include things such as a minimum and maximum percentage of contributions to discussions that each individual must make, or guidelines regarding (in)appropriate language in electronic discussion rooms.

2   Find out what the assessment criteria are, what marks will be awarded for meeting each of the criteria and if there are any penalties for lack of participation, or for deliberately jeopardising the success of a project.

3   Ensure that the group sets out a clear list of tasks, with the name(s) of those responsible for completing the tasks and the time schedule for doing so.

4   Suggest (if it hasn't been done by your tutor) that for different group projects different people assume different roles and that these roles are recorded at the start of each project. For example: the chairperson takes responsibility for encouraging other members and ensuring that every member makes their contribution; the project manager records the schedule for the project and checks that all tasks are completed on time; the purchase or resources manager ensures that all resources are available for the appropriate stage of the project; and so on.

5   Share any anxieties about group-working or about a specific project with the group, but beware of turning a discussion into a moaning session rather than focusing on the work itself.

6   Don't get too upset if people disagree with you: it is very stimulating, if you can avoid being too defensive, to have your own views challenged by others. It is best seen as an opportunity to learn of other people's perspectives on a subject. At times you will have the thrill that comes from letting go and taking on new views and beliefs. At other times it can ultimately be reassuring, having listened with an open mind to others' perspectives, to conclude that you still hold the same view and to feel that you have satisfactorily 'defended' it.

Group members working effectively together form a valuable resource that can be tapped by each individual member. Whilst you may not feel that you have a great deal to offer for every activity, there will be times when your contribution might be one of the most significant. Remember that working with others is all about 'give and take' and mutual support. Some frustration is probably inevitable from time to time, but hopefully the overall experience will be very positive.

7.2 Reading

Since so much time on a course of study is spent reading, it is crucial that none of that time is wasted. It is essential that you:

- Read with a purpose
- Read selectively
- Read critically and analytically

Doing background reading before the start of a course or by way of preparation for an essay can sometimes be seen as an overwhelming experience, largely due to the enormous amount of information that is available. The task can be made more manageable if you start with introductory texts on a subject, or use secondary sources such as a review article where the literature of a subject is discussed. Some students are fortunate enough to be given an annotated bibliography or reading list at the start of their course, which instantly provides more information about each item on the list. The purpose here is to help you to familiarise yourself in general terms with the subject and to learn some new vocabulary. Not everyone is this lucky though and you need to develop your own strategies for deciding what you want (or need) to read. No one will be this 'spoon-fed' throughout their course in any case, and certainly when it comes to researching for an assignment, some of the marks are likely to be awarded for evidence of your ability to select relevant literature and other sources yourself. (The information provided in Chapter 6 and Section 8.2 will help you do this.)

Relevance

With the help of catalogues, indexes and abstracts and the development of good searching strategies, you will eventually find what you hope are relevant items of literature and electronic sources to read.

However, once you finally have the item on the desk or PC in front of you, it is worth spending a few minutes employing the following strategies to confirm that it is going to be worth spending many more minutes, or even hours, reading a particular book or article which could turn out to be unsuitable after all. Try to put yourself into a questioning frame of mind by asking questions such as: Why am I interested in this item? How will it contribute to my essay / assignment / group work preparation?

It is not recommended that you set out to read an academic book from cover to cover. Even if it turns out that the book is very relevant to your studies, you will get far more out of it if you find out a bit more about it first.

Cover

Read the dust jacket or back cover of a book. Although this is provided by the publisher primarily to encourage sales, it can also provide a useful indication of its overall relevance to your needs. It tells you about the author – their standing in the academic community, their qualifications for writing the book and their contribution to a particular field.

Abstract

An abstract at the start of a journal article or of an item on a website is likely to be more informative than a book cover. In the case of academic journals the abstract should conform to the protocol of academic writing and provide an accurate, brief account of what is in the article. Indeed you may have obtained the article only after reading an abstract in a database, but if you have come across it via an index or search engine or by browsing through a journal it is well worth reading the abstract first. An abstract will provide information such as how the item adds to the body of knowledge, what methodology was used in any research, and the main conclusions.

Contents

Read the contents page of a book or website so that you can select only the relevant chapters / sections or even a few pages, using the chapter / section sub-headings to guide you.

Index

Scan the index of a book for appropriate or relevant vocabulary. If none of the terms used there are familiar to you (for example the words that are used in an essay title) it may be that the book isn't worth reading after all. An index can also provide an overview of the key concepts covered in a book and help you build up an idea of the structure of a subject.

Bibliography

Scan the bibliography to see if you recognise some of the references. Once you become familiar with your subject area you will come to know at least a handful of authors that you would expect to see there.

Introduction

Read the introduction to a book. This can sometimes be the author's preface or it may be the first chapter. In the case of a collection of essays or papers that have been put together by an academic editor the introduction will be especially useful, since the key points of each chapter usually will have been picked out by the editor. The introduction may also give you an idea of the author's point of view or perspective on the subject of the book, which will help you to read critically and analytically.

Conclusion

Read the final chapter of the book. It's not like reading the end of a novel when you don't want to know what happens. In fact the opposite is true: you want to read a summary by the author of what has gone before or read the overall conclusions that they have reached by the end of the book, to know if you want to read the detail. As with the introduction, the conclusion will provide a rich source of information to enable critical and analytical reading.

Chapters

Use scanning and skimming to delve into chapters to assess how much of each chapter to read. Read the first and last paragraphs of a chapter and read the first and last sentences of a few other paragraphs.

Double check

Don't just rely on one of the above strategies in isolation. You will need to employ two or three to ensure that you don't reject something potentially useful.

Take stock

Some people find it helpful to start a mind map or spider diagram at this point, before progressing to the more in-depth stages of reading. (See the section on the design of notes later in this chapter for more on mind maps.) This involves noting down the keywords for the knowledge you have gained from your reading up to this point. This can make your reading from now on faster and more effective.

An example of what the core part of a mind map might look like is given in Figure 7.1 for the essay title shown there. You will see that this first version of the mind map covers only the key concepts from the first part of the question. These have been arrived at after some

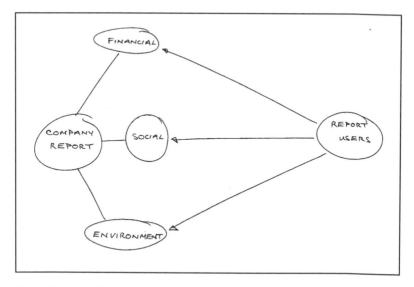

Figure 7.1   Mind map 1

Note: Essay title: 'Identify and explain the major classifications of company information required by users. Outline the reports typically required by various types of user, justifying your linkages.'

preliminary reading around the subject. Figure 7.2 in Section 7.3 shows the more developed version of the mind map in response to the second part of the essay title, after more detailed reading has taken place.

Order of reading

If, after employing the previous strategies, you decide that you will read some or all of the book or article, don't assume that you need to read the chapters or sections in the order that they are provided. This is especially true of edited collections of different papers. Where the book is by a single author, however, it may be possible that they develop a theme or argument as the book progresses (rather like a good essay – see Section 7.5), in which case you will only get confused if you don't read in a logical order. You should have been able to find out whether or not this is likely to be the case by following the suggested earlier strategies. A lot of information on websites is not intended to be read in a linear way (indeed the flexibility of access to information via the web is one of its assets), but beware of getting lost by going off to other, less relevant, sites. A good website will help you keep track of where you are by providing helpful navigation tools.

Speed reading

Once you have identified that a chapter is relevant, one strategy you could employ rather than reading each section thoroughly (as below) to begin with, is first to read the chapter rapidly several times, building up a picture of what each section is about.

Critical and analytical reading

Whatever order you eventually decide to read a book in, try not to be tempted to simply read what's written, passively accepting everything that's there. To do so is a bit like watching a television programme without listening to the sound. When we read we need to really engage with the writer and 'hear' what the author is saying. To do this we need to stop and think from time to time about what we have just read and consider whether or not, and in what respects, we agree with it or believe it to be based on sound evidence. In other words we need to make a considered response to what we've read. It is a good idea to employ the tactic of double reading: first doing a quick skim of the page, or several pages, to get the gist of what is being said; and then returning for a second reading, going over the content much more carefully and making notes on the key points as you go. It is also useful to note your response to what you have read at these key places.

If you are to read critically and analytically you need to compare different points of view that are presented in different books and articles and to be able to make judgements about what is being said. You can start to make judgements by asking the following questions about something that you are reading:

- How much of what is written is fact and how much is opinion?
- Where the author expresses an opinion, is it backed up with evidence or is it simply their latest idea?
- Where evidence is cited, is it recent evidence?
- Does the author have a lot of experience in this particular field?
- Are the author's conclusions based on what is written earlier?
- What are the logical outcomes of following that person's point of view or belief? Are they reasonable and desirable?
- Can you identify the 'school of thought' of the author?
- Does anyone else in the field oppose the author's view?

Activity Twenty-Two

You may be able, at this point, to add to the above list, giving some of your own examples of how to read critically and analytically in your particular subject area.

Note your response

Just because an author has been published does not mean that everything written in a book or journal is academically sound or conforms to current thinking on a subject. That said, academic publishers will always have commissioned peer review of the content before publishing. It is nevertheless possible to question what is written, especially if it is not supported by evidence. However, it is important not to be a lone voice disagreeing with several academically renowned authors who agree with one another. Challenging the accepted wisdom of a specific subject is generally reserved for doctoral or post-doctoral study!

It is especially important to make judgements about what you read on web pages, since there is often no academic publisher involved to give credence to what is published on the web. (See Section 8.3 for a checklist of how to critically evaluate websites.) In particular check out the academic credentials of the author of the materials. The material written by most academics and found on the web will be on sites produced by their academic institution or by the organisers of conferences where papers have been presented. The clue is often very simply in the URL of the website.

Stopping reading

It is important to recognise when to stop reading. This will be when the items you are reading are not providing you with any new material and / or your research questions have been answered.

A note on academic criticism

Criticism in general terms is regarded as something negative, but in an academic context it has a rather different meaning. Criticism does not have to imply negativity; rather it is an opportunity to state what is good about something too. Where something isn't good, it is constructive if you can point out precisely what is wrong and in what ways it could be improved. As you will read later in this chapter, constructive criticism of your essays by your tutors is to be welcomed (even though it might not initially feel like it!). If you are able to develop a critical and analytical approach to listening, thinking and reading you will be better equipped to write critically and analytically.

Academic criticism is fully accepted as a crucial component of study in higher education at institutions in most parts of the world. In particular, if you are registered for a course with an institution in the UK or other European country, in the USA, Canada or Australia, you will be expected to adopt this approach. This may be difficult for you to do at first if you have a different cultural background, but be assured that it will not be interpreted as a rude, personal insult on the author when you include academic criticism in your essays or your contributions to online or face to face discussions.

7.3 Note making from reading

It is crucial to make notes from your reading as it assists the mind to engage with the material and to process what you have read. People's choice of how they make notes varies considerably. However, although it is quite a personal activity, the following strategies have worked for many.

Highlighting

If you are the sort of person who likes to mark key passages of what you are reading by using a highlighter pen, by writing in the margins or underlining, you will need to make photocopies of the relevant pages of books and journals or make printouts from electronic sources. Never make notes on a library copy of a book or journal.

Copyright

Of course, you need to ensure that the material you are photocopying falls within the limits of what you are allowed to copy for personal use under the terms of the current law on copyright. The licence agreement of the institution where you are doing the copying will usually be displayed near the photocopier.

Additional notes

If you need to write more notes than will fit into the margins of the photocopies, it is a good idea to use a card or a piece of paper and to staple this to the photocopied article. In this way you ensure that you keep all the notes together.

Physical means

You may choose to record your notes on cards or sheets of paper or you may want to input them directly onto a PC. The latter, though time consuming, means that you may later be able to use some of your notes in the body of your essay without repeating the writing activity, but there is a danger then of including everything you have collected, just because it's there.

Summarise your thoughts

In making the initial notes, don't be tempted to write down every-thing you have read. Rather read through a section at a time, think about it, then write a brief summary of what you have read in your own words, checking the original text for accurate spelling of new words and to record the names of people, and so on.

Design

You may choose to make notes in a linear fashion or using some kind of pictorial representation of your ideas. Those who are more visual according to the VARK categories of learning preferences (Fleming and Bonwell 2001) will probably find the latter more appealing (see Section 2.8 for details). Some people make linear notes initially as they read through source materials, then they read their notes and produce some form of mind map or spider diagram from them, pick-ing out the key points / themes and highlighting them. This involves writing down the main theme drawn from your reading in the centre of the page and drawing connecting lines from there to other relevant ideas, as well as lines to show the connections between the various ideas. This has the added advantage of helping you to absorb or digest what you have been reading and to start to think about your response to it.

An example of what a mind map might look like is given in Figure 7.2. It is a more detailed version of the one given in Figure 7.1 in Section 7.2. It is based on the essay title shown. You will see that in Figure 7.2 the more extensive mind map indicates the development of the concepts in response to the second part of the essay title, after further reading has taken place.

To use or not to use

After reading and note making you should consider splitting the cop-ies of any articles / chapters and sets of notes into different categories: those that you definitely want to use; those that you might possibly use; and those that you reject. It is better to discard irrelevant material

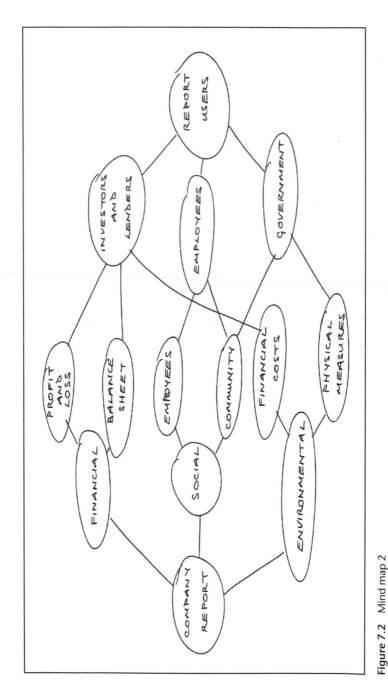

Figure 7.2 Mind map 2

Note: Essay title: 'Identify and explain the major classifications of company information required by users. Outline the reports typically required by various types of user, justifying your linkages.'

at this stage than be tempted to include everything in your essay just because you have it. If you've made notes directly onto your computer, you may have some deleting to do at this stage. If you're not quite sure, create another version of your data file with a new file name, so that if you change your mind, you can retrieve your work.

7.4 Recording and using sources

Bibliographical details

At the start of any reading and note making session, record the full bibliographical details of the item you are about to read, if you don't already have them from the literature searching stage, and the source of the item (library, website and so on). You could do this on index cards but if you have the opportunity it is much better to use some form of software to record the details on a PC. This could simply be done in Word or some other word processing program, but specialist software is available specifically to record bibliographical details (see Section 8.2 for details of *Endnote* and *Reference Manager* software). Whichever means you use to record the details it is advisable to use the Harvard system of referencing so that you gradually build up your bibliography in the course of researching and reading for your essay (see Section 8.8 for details of referencing). However, the choice of referencing system will be determined by your institution and may even vary from one department to another within the same institution. Check their guidelines at an early stage.

At the top of each page of notes write the author, date and title of the item, so that you have a clear record of the source of your notes.

Cite your sources / plagiarism

Be meticulous about citing and referencing your sources and quotes. Plagiarism (that is taking and using another person's thoughts or writings as your own) is not allowed. You may have a whole assignment or examination disallowed if you do plagiarise another person's work. You may even be dismissed from your whole programme of study. The penalties for plagiarism at your institution are likely to be laid out in the college or university student handbook. Copying is not allowed from paper or web sources. There is sophisticated software available for institutions to use to check mechanically whether your work contains material from websites.

Sometimes plagiarism can be unintentional, in the sense that you forget to cite the source. However, in many institutions this excuse does not constitute an acceptable defence and you would still suffer the consequences.

Quotations

If you decide that a short section of the original text of a book or article is going to provide a really useful quote in your essay, be especially meticulous about recording your sources. You can spend hours returning to the library to rediscover the exact page number of a quote. Don't, however, let your essay become just a series of quotes. If an author expresses something very clearly it is reasonable to quote them, but you have to explain in your own words why the quote is relevant to the essay and how it supports your own reasoning. Even when you are not quoting an author verbatim you should acknowledge the source of ideas / evidence / theories to which you refer in the text of your essays.

There are various ways of laying out long and short passages of text. Again guidance may well be provided by your department, and there are also guides such as those referred to in Section 8.8 that help you do this.

7.5 Essay writing

Although the style of writing required to complete all of your assignments is likely to vary during the course and may include reports, observations, numerical or scientific exercises, case studies and essays, it is often the writing of traditional essays that creates most anxiety amongst students. This is especially true of those who are returning to study after a gap of some years. I am, therefore, going to concentrate on essays in this section. Most of you reading this book have probably done some sort of study in further or higher education in the past and have therefore written essays before. What follows is a reminder list of strategies to help you plan and write successful essays. Some of the more general strategies suggested are applicable to all assignments, irrespective of the form of writing needed. Some strategies will apply to writing essays for unseen written examinations as well as to writing essays submitted throughout the course. Clearly, however, some aspects, such as asking someone else to read a draft to check that you have made yourself understood, are luxuries not afforded in the examination environment!

Created not born

Remember that you are not born a good essay writer. Rather you develop into one – but only through:

- Reflecting on your strengths and weaknesses
- Gaining feedback to use in that reflection
- Using resources such as this book, people and computers to tackle your weaknesses
- Using checklists
- Giving your reading and writing plenty of time
- Reflecting often on what you have written

Start early

Allow plenty of time to research and write each essay – a good essay will take many hours of reading, note making and writing. If you leave it too close to the deadline you will be too pressured to do a good job and you are likely to find that the key books that you need to read will already have been requested by others from the university or college library. As with other aspects of your studies, you need to plan backwards from the deadline for each assignment and add to your chart when you need to start your literature searching for each one. (See the Gantt chart, Figure 4.1 in Section 4.6.)

Assessment criteria

Find out what the assessment criteria are for your assignment / essay / report and how many or what percentage of marks are allocated to each criterion. Depending on the subject, some tutors award marks for good spelling / punctuation / grammar or conversely subtract marks if these aspects of an essay are poor. Most (or all) marks are likely to be awarded for your ability to:

- Express your ideas clearly
- Provide evidence that you have conducted sufficient research, that is read widely and deeply about the subject
- Show that you can analyse and critically appraise what you have read
- Present and justify your own argument and conclusions

How many words?

Take note of the minimum and maximum word allowance for each piece of work.

Read the question

Some tutors (examiners) are more helpful than others in the way they formulate essay / assignment questions. However it is worded, read and re-read the question and break it down into various component parts if it is complicated. Pick out the keywords from the title. Add your own words and phrases as you think through exactly what is being asked in the question. These words and phrases will help you in your literature search. Include the full range of concepts you will need to cover.

Read the literature

Perform your literature search for the assignment and obtain useful books and articles. (Chapter 6 and Section 8.2 will help you do this.) Don't forget to check reading lists from your tutor where such lists have been provided. The length of the assignment and the marks allocated to it will largely determine the time you spend on your literature search and the number of items it is necessary to obtain and read to meet the assessment criteria. Don't be tempted to try to read everything there is on a subject – each assignment is not a research project. Although you will probably have some materials provided by your tutor(s) that are relevant to the title of the essay, tutors don't want simply to receive back a re-ordered version of these materials. They want to see that you have been thinking about the information they have given you and developing your ideas. It is also important that you show you have read more widely than the notes they have given you.

Make notes

It is important that you make notes from the literature as you read it. How you might do this was explored in Section 7.3. Ensure that you record all of the bibliographical details of everything you read, especially the page numbers of any phrases or short passages you may want to quote verbatim.

Make a plan

Plan your essay before you start to write the substance. Note down keywords or features / ideas / arguments you want to make, and the reference(s) you want to use to support those ideas. This has sometimes been known as 'brainstorming' or, more recently 'thoughtstorming' your ideas. Don't worry about the order of these individual points initially. Again people vary in the way they find it helpful to note down their essay ideas, just as they do in making notes on their reading. Some will write in a linear way, whilst others will use mind maps or spider diagrams. The latter has the advantage of showing the relationship between the main points, and may ultimately help you decide on the order in which you will write about these points in your essay. In practice your mind map will be developed during the combined tasks of planning your essay and doing the background reading for it. (See Figure 7.2 in Section 7.3 for an example.) Re-read the essay question and ensure that you have ideas that address each part of it.

Make your points

Expand each of the keywords or features into one or two paragraphs, commenting critically and analytically on what you have read and citing the sources. Keep reminding yourself of the question / essay title and check that what you are writing is relevant. Write concisely and succinctly, yet using enough words to be able to summarise unambiguously the theories and / or the arguments in what you have read, and to express your own opinions and ideas.

Link it all together

Put the various paragraphs into a logical order and write the linking text. This is the point at which the disjointed parts come together to form a coherent whole. It is also where you gradually develop your line of reasoned argument throughout the essay. It is in writing the linking text that you may well decide to change the order of the different parts of the essay or to re-write some of the paragraphs to make more sense in view of the developing argument. Writing down everything you have learned about a subject does not constitute a good essay – you *must* answer the question. Sometimes what you leave out is as important as what you leave in.

Conclusion

Draw your conclusions based on the points you have made earlier, combining sound evidence from your reading with some original thoughts of your own.

Introduction

The introduction is very often the last thing to be written, providing as it does an outline of what is to follow and a hint of what your conclusions are.

Use of first person

It has traditionally been accepted in most academic subjects that we avoid using the word 'I' in academic writing when expressing our views. This has been seen as a way of encouraging you to focus on the argument and the evidence. However, the rules seem to be changing and now vary from one academic discipline to another. Reflective writing in particular requires that you personalise it, so the rules will change depending upon the nature of the assignment. It is worth checking out at the start of your course what the accepted practice is for your subject and for different types of work.

Use plain English

Don't be tempted to use long words or complicated sentences in the essay: they do not equate with intellectual ability – often the opposite is true. The ability to write clearly and understandably is far more impressive!

Understand what you write

Don't use words that you don't understand. If you come across a word or phrase in a reading that you want to quote, ensure that you understand its meaning before using it. Your tutor or other students may ask you about it in a discussion of your essay.

Use drafts

You will need to write more than one draft. Once again, the number of marks allocated to a particular assignment will help determine just how much time you spend on this task and therefore how many versions you will produce, but there comes a point when you have to stop and be prepared to submit it. (Often the deadline will impose this discipline in any case.) Word processing packages on PCS are wonderful (especially the spell-checker!) and it may be possible that you are constantly amending your copy as you work through your document. However it is a good idea to stop at some point and print off a full draft. Leave it for a while (preferably until the next day) and return to it with a more detached and self-critical approach to what you have written. Make final amendments.

Reviewers

If possible ask someone not on your course to read and review a fairly advanced draft of your work to ensure that they can understand what you have written. Clearly with higher-level courses a non-specialist will not be able to understand all of the meaning, but they may be able to point out, for example, where your argument has not been presented in a clear and logical way. Whilst it would be wrong for someone else to actually contribute to your work, it is generally accepted practice that others are allowed to view your drafts and to point out where more evidence is required or when some references are not provided. For some assignments the tutors themselves may be prepared to read your draft and give advice before you submit the final version. Write down the feedback and use it as a reminder for other essays.

Read the feedback

For some programmes of study you will be writing essays at various points throughout your course and before a final examination or assignment. This is sometimes called formative assessment and may or may not count towards the final mark for your course. In such cases the feedback you receive from your tutor who reads your essay is almost as important as the mark itself. Good feedback will be supportive, giving constructive criticism of your essay and providing advice on how to improve your performance in your next essay. If you don't understand any of the feedback provided by your tutor, don't be afraid to ask for clarification, or even to question or challenge it. Discussion of your work is good – it will help you see how to improve it and it will help you to recognise where and how to make your argument more clearly.

Your tutor may also suggest key readings that you have not discovered for yourself. Don't be tempted just to look at the mark and be relieved that you have passed – read the feedback. The process of writing an essay and reading the feedback is as much a part of learning as reading study materials or attending lectures. As was stated in Section 2.4, the principal purpose of formative assessment is development rather than judgement.

When writing your next essay get out the feedback on previous essays and use it as a checklist – especially to spot your spelling and grammar mistakes.

Practice for exams

Every time you prepare for and write an essay it is good practice for writing examination answers. The key points of reading the question, doing a plan and linking your points together to develop your argument are all crucial elements of writing good examination answers. These combined with taking heed of the feedback received are all essential preparation for final exams. Effort put into writing essays will be rewarded two-fold – in the marks received for the essay itself and in the marks received in an exam.

More help

For further advice on writing, citations and referencing see Section 8.8 on report writing, in Chapter 8. Your department or university / college may also issue its own guidelines. See also the details of other resources at the end of this book. If you require more than a reminder about writing essays and need more in-depth advice about the process, an excellent book is Creme and Lea (2003). Another is Rose (2001). (See Guides to reading and writing in Further Resources for details.)

7.6 Revising for examinations

Although many tutors are now choosing to use more innovative forms of assessment (including electronic means) and are providing continuous assessment throughout the course, a lot of importance is still attached by many to the final written examination at the end of a module or full programme of study.

Even where assignments have been submitted by post or electronic mail at regular intervals through your course, many distance learners are expected to attend a final examination in person, not least to satisfy your study institution's requirements regarding authentication / identity of the registered students. Even if you don't have to attend your host institution you are likely to be asked to sit an unseen written examination paper at a local study centre.

Whilst some people thrive in such a situation and welcome the opportunity to demonstrate all that they have learned, the vast majority of us do not readily embrace the prospect of final exams, and the pressure and concentrated period of effort associated with them. Nevertheless, with a little forethought and a calm approach, the experience does not have to be quite as traumatic as many would have us believe. The key to being successful in exams is good preparation for them, namely – revision.

The skills required for the combined process of revision and sitting exams are essentially those that have already been addressed in this chapter so far – reading, making notes and writing. In addition, whilst it is not something everyone (especially distance learners) have the chance or desire to do, some people also use their skills of working with others to help them to prepare for exams. Some people find it helpful to revise with one or more other person and / or to have someone test them before their exams by asking them questions.

Planning

Whilst serious planning for revision and exams is naturally going to begin towards the end of your module, there is a sense in which planning needs to begin right at the start of it. If you are organised in the way you make and store notes from your reading and from any lectures you might attend, this will make your task of revising a little easier. Filing together all material related to each topic being covered on your course means that you know where to find it all when you come to revise.

When to revise

Well before the actual period of revision needs to begin, you need to make a revision diary or chart. You need to note on this a timetable or a schedule of the weeks over which you will revise and what topics you will revise in which weeks or days. Similarly, just as you have to decide as a distance learner at what time of day or night you are going to do your studying and complete your assignments, you need to consider realistically when you are going to find time in your week to revise.

Activity Twenty-Three

Although you may already have done a study schedule and a weekly planner for your whole programme of study, it is probably a good idea to do separate and more detailed versions of these for the period of revision. Clearly this will be an activity to which you will return once you know more about the exact nature of your course, and if and when any exams of this sort are scheduled. Remember though that the key to time management is knowing when to amend your schedule.

The overall period of time that you devote to revision and how many weeks ahead of the exams you begin to revise is going to be something for you to work out for yourself. Some people are very systematic and start some revision many weeks before the exams; others find that if they start too early they can't remember everything on the day. However, I would advise that you don't leave it too late to begin: most people find they don't leave enough time. If you follow the strategy for revision suggested later in this section, you will hopefully find that you can do the different stages of revision over an extended period of time and ultimately discover that you can recall it all.

What to revise

The best advice to give is that you should revise everything included in each module on your programme. However, as a part-time student you may need to be strategic in your choice of revision topics, especially if you know that it is unrealistic to revise every element of your course. However, deciding which topics to revise and which ones to set aside is a very risky business. Another approach that is used by some students is to revise most but not all topics in greater depth, and to revise the remaining topics to a lesser extent. This at least means that if you really do have to answer a question on a topic that you hadn't really anticipated you would not be completely devoid of ideas. Your own interests, and your strengths and weaknesses, will also help you to decide which topics need most work, which ones you should tackle and which ones to avoid if possible. You may even get some hints from lecturers, so don't miss out on any online discussions or face to face elements of the course as examinations draw closer.

Whilst not foolproof, you can often see from past exam papers which topics always or nearly always come up for a particular module. Looking at past papers also helps you to become familiar with the structure of the paper: how many questions have to be answered; which ones are compulsory; and so on. (Of course this can change from year to year, so always read the instructions on the top of your paper when the time comes.)

Reading

Revision essentially consists of doing a lot of reading and trying to absorb what you read in order to be able to reproduce the ideas, points of view, theories and so on in a written examination. It doesn't often mean committing to memory in a rote-learning sense, but in the case of mathematical or scientific formulae or passages of literature, for example, you may have no choice but to do so. How each individual does this varies a great deal, but for most of us repetition is a major element of the process.

What you should read will vary according to your particular course. For some courses the tutor will make it clear that if you thoroughly know all that is in a detailed study manual or included in online learning materials you will be well prepared. For most courses, though, you will also need to re-read your own essays or other assignments and even some of the articles or extracts from books that you used to prepare to write those assignments. If you have made and kept good summary notes of your topics as you worked through the module or as you prepared an assignment, use these as a starting point for your revision.

Making notes

Most people find that it helps to make notes when they are revising. This can ensure that revision reading becomes a more active rather than simply passive activity. As with note making when reading as you prepare to write an essay, it is better to read a section at a time, think about what you have read, and only then make notes that summarise what you have read, using whatever style of writing that best suits you and your subject. Again, as when preparing for essay writing, try as a second stage to reduce the longer version of your notes to some diagrammatic form, or simply a list of related topics. (A diagram is easier for showing the relationship between elements.) Finally, extract a few keywords or phrases from each list or diagram and commit these to memory – by rote, if necessary. Hopefully (if you have done the revision thoroughly in the earlier stages) by recalling these keywords in the examination room, you will remember the diagram in your head, which in turn will lead to a whole chain reaction of thought, and you will find that all the knowledge that you need will be 'unlocked'.

It is probably better to go through each of the three stages of note making in different weeks if possible, and certainly on different days within your revision schedule. This way you are revisiting the subject at regular intervals and 'topping up' the store of knowledge in your head. Some people, however, prefer to go through all three stages in one sitting for each topic, returning to the keywords a day or two before the exam, just to refresh their memory.

7.7 Sitting examinations

I have already suggested towards the end of Section 7.5 that each essay or other form of assignment you write during your course is practice for your exams. Although the timing is of course far more restricted in the exam situation, which puts you under more pressure, the process of writing the answers is essentially the same as when writing for assignments. Some exams are even open book exams, where you don't have to rely completely on your memory to recall crucial information, and the examiner is looking for your appropriate interpretation of the data rather than your recall of them. It needs to be said, however, that this type of exam is still relatively rare. Whatever form your exam is going to take there are some steps you can take beforehand to ensure that you are able to do your best.

Assessment criteria

Although you are unlikely to receive a list of assessment criteria for each exam question, it is not unreasonable to ask your tutor well ahead of the exam for a list of criteria that they will, in general terms, be applying when marking the exam answers. These are likely to be similar to those provided for each of your assignments, but there could be some differences so it's worth checking this out.

Handwriting / spelling / grammar

Exam markers are likely to be a bit more lenient about these than they would be in marking an assignment prepared in more time and with the use of a word processor. However, whilst you are not going to get extra marks added for neatness you may lose marks if the examiner cannot understand your answer because of these factors. No examiner is going to spend very long struggling to try and work out what you mean by something you have written in an exam answer, if it is not immediately clear.

Planning for the exam

You should be aware well before an exam of how much time you will be allowed in total and how many questions you will have to answer in that time. It is therefore possible to have decided beforehand how much time you can devote to answering each question. Don't be tempted to simply divide the total time by the number of questions, say three hours by four questions, which makes 45 minutes per question. It is advisable to allow, say, ten minutes at the start of the exam to read through the whole paper and decide which questions you are going to answer (where there is a choice) and the order that you might prefer to answer them in. You should also try to allow another ten minutes before the end of the exam to read through your answers, and check for and correct any errors that it is easy to make when you are writing at speed in exam conditions. So, subtracting 20 minutes from the total leaves you in fact with 160 minutes or only 40 minutes per question.

Beforehand

Some people can stay calmer than others at the time of exams. Although you will need to check your keywords the day or night before, it is best not to be revising for too many hours immediately before an exam. Instead, try to relax, perhaps by doing some form of physical exercise, followed by a soak in the bath, and try to get an early night.

On the day of the exam, try to allow plenty of time to travel to the exam centre. You don't want to arrive hot and flustered after rushing there, and you certainly don't want to be late – you may not be allowed to sit the exam at all, which would be a great waste of all that effort. If you have never been to the exam centre before and you are not sure where it is, it is probably a good idea to travel there on a previous occasion, if it is not too expensive or time-consuming to do so. Once you know exactly where it is, it is one less thing to worry about as the day of your exam approaches.

Remember to take with you whatever writing, mathematical or scientific instruments you are going to need, as well as your college or university identification card and / or exam entrance number, which may be needed to gain access to the exam centre. You may also need the details of the exact room number where your exam is taking place.

Don't allow others to make you nervous before the exam – if necessary wait away from the crowd. Similarly, don't analyse the paper at length afterwards.

Write your name or number

Most exams are now taken anonymously, so you will need to take with you your examination entry number or code and write this in the appropriate place on the exam script or cover sheet, whichever system is used by your institution. It would be a nightmare if, after doing so much work before and during an exam, you were not given credit for your answers.

Read the whole paper

Even if you think you know how long the paper is due to last and how many questions you have to answer, always read the instructions at the top of each exam paper before you start. It's very easy in a stressful situation to misremember the more straightforward things. Check too if there is any choice on the paper – you don't always have to answer all of the questions. Take care here as sometimes you have to answer a set number of questions from each section of the paper or all questions from section one and three more from the rest of the paper. Take your time and recalculate, if necessary, how many minutes you definitely have for each question, allowing yourself time at the beginning and at the end of the whole paper, as suggested above.

Take note too of any instructions about using the answer sheets. In most exams you are expected to start your answer to each question on a new sheet of paper. This is usually so that different people can mark individual questions at the same time.

Read through all of the questions and make a mental or preferably a written note as you read through the paper about which ones you think you could answer most successfully. Note too if you think you could answer two or three better than the others and decide the order in which you are going to do them. Beware, if you don't write your answers in the same order in which the questions are set, that you don't forget to return to an earlier one and realise with horror after the exam that you didn't answer the required number of questions. Write at the top of the paper which ones you decide to tackle. Put the numbers clearly on your first sheet.

Read each question

Having decided upon the questions you are going to answer and the order in which you are going to do them, read through each question twice before starting to plan your answer, and again from time to time *as* you write your answer. As you read through the question the second time, pick out the component parts and note them down separately or divide up the question with oblique strokes on the question paper.

Planning each answer

Keep in mind how much time you have for each answer, but allow the first five minutes or so to plan each answer. This will be time well spent.

As when planning an essay, note down the key elements that need to be included in your answer, thinking about the relationship between the elements and the order in which you want to include them in your answer. If it is an essay type answer, jot down the key-words that you need to include in your conclusion. Even where it is not an essay answer still note down the key parts that you need to include in your answer so that you don't forget to complete all parts of it.

Writing your answer

Unlike when writing an essay in a non-exam situation, you are going to have to write your introduction right at the start of your answer for an exam. But unlike when you are writing an essay, you already know the subject matter, you have noted down what to include and how to conclude the answer. Once you have these you are ready to write the introduction and thereafter to continue into the body of your answer.

When writing an essay-type answer in an exam you don't have time to have the luxury of writing the component parts and then rearranging them. That's why your plan is so important. Hopefully you will have collected your thoughts together at that stage and you can be confident of writing your answer in the time available, in a logical and well argued way. You will be able to show, not just what you know, but that you are capable of using that knowledge in an appropriate and well structured way.

Tick off each part of your notes when you have written about a particular topic and at the end of writing your answer put a line through the whole of your notes for that question. Rules will vary according to who has set the exam, but generally you are expected to hand in everything you have written in the course of the exam, even if you don't want it to be seen as part of your final answer. You need to ensure that it is very clear which part of the script contains your notes and which is your final answer.

As well as planning the content of your answer, you need to think about how much time you will spend writing about each aspect of the answer. Although you don't want to spend too many valuable minutes on the planning stage, it is probably wise to jot down very quickly on your plan before you start writing how many minutes you intend to use for writing each part, so that the sum of the parts is not greater than the time available for answering that one question. You need to be constantly aware of the time as you are writing. Even if you don't have time to include all aspects that you had intended, it is better to ensure that you have written your concluding argument at the end of an essay, or come up with a solution at the end of an answer that involves calculations or theories.

That said, marks are often awarded for the processes involved in completing calculations, even if the final solution is not accurate in every respect, so don't be tempted to cross out your workings if you feel that the solution is not correct. Again, any rough workings or notes that ultimately you don't want to be considered, should be clearly crossed out.

If it looks like you are going to run out of time, ensure that you have made an attempt at as many of the required number of questions as you can. Remember it is always harder to get the last 30 percent of the marks for a question than it is to get the first 30 percent. Avoid perfecting your answers and not leaving yourself enough time to attempt all the questions that you need to.

At the end of the exam

Ideally there should be ten minutes left after you have finished answering your last question to skim read all of your answers.

Although this isn't enough time to amend anything you discover that is seriously wrong, it does give you time to spot minor errors in spelling or use of words or phrases or calculations and to put them right. You could pick up a few extra marks this way – marks that could make the difference between passing the exam and not doing so.

Summary of Chapter 7

In this chapter you have:

- Had the opportunity to revisit some of the basic study skills you will probably need to successfully complete your distance learning course
- Considered how to make the most of any group working experience you may have
- Given particular thought to how to read and write critically and analytically in your particular subject area

8 Doing your research project

Introduction

Conducting a research project and writing the research report or dissertation is likely to be the largest single piece of academic work that you do for your programme of study, especially if you are studying at masters level. It will dominate your course (and most aspects of your life) for at least the second half of your period of study. As with all other aspects of your studies, planning ahead for your research project will reap major benefits. Time spent beforehand exploring your ideas for research and the feasibility and practicalities of putting your ideas into practice will be time well spent.

This chapter does not attempt to provide everything you need to know about doing research (indeed it will barely scratch the surface) but there are many excellent and comprehensive books available to help you. Some of these are included in the Further Resources and References sections at the end of this book. In particular this chapter does not look at specific methodologies or techniques for actually doing the research. Rather it is an attempt to provide the practical framework within which you will need to work to conduct and report on your research successfully. I do hope that by working through this chapter at an early stage in your studies and considering some of the issues raised, you will be better prepared for the task ahead and will be able to avoid some of the pitfalls in doing research that can be both painful and very time consuming to tumble into. You may well wish to return to some parts of the chapter at a later stage in your programme of study when you have had time to get to know your subject better and have received some initial guidance from your course leader.

Whilst there are obviously some added difficulties in conducting research when you are at a distance from your study institution, the continual development of resources on the web means that you are less disadvantaged than distance learners used to be in this task. Access to bibliographical resources will to some extent depend upon the subscriptions paid by your institution for off-campus access, for example to electronic journals and so on. However, as already indicated in Chapter 6, there is a lot available electronically to assist you in your studies. The section on using the web for research later in the present chapter provides you with even more ideas on the ways in which the web might be utilised.

All of us feel somewhat daunted at the prospect of embarking upon a research project, especially when approaching the task for the first time. There is nothing for it but to breathe deeply, relax, keep a clear head, listen to advice from others and *begin*. We start this chapter with a brief consideration of exactly what research is and why you are doing it.

8.1 Preparing to do research

What is research?

It is not easy to give one universally accepted definition of research, though there is a consensus on what is its general nature.

Activity Twenty-Four

Make a list of what *you* consider academic research to be. You may find it helpful to consider how doing academic research differs from researching for say a novel or a newspaper article. One example of what academic research is might be: *a process by which to test a hypothesis.*

> *Note your response*

Commentary

You may have included some of the following ideas:

- A means of checking assumed knowledge for validity
- A way of collecting accurate factual information
- The analysis of data
- An attempt to discover the truth
- A way of gathering new knowledge
- A means of deepening our understanding

Phillips and Pugh (2000) distinguish research from what they call 'intelligence gathering' (p. 46). They emphasise that research is concerned with more than answering the *what* questions. 'Research goes beyond description and requires analysis. It looks for explanations, relationships, comparisons, predictions, generalisations and theories. These are the *why* questions. (pp. 47–8).

For a more detailed commentary on the nature of research see Blaxter *et al.* (2001: ch. 1).

The research process will vary considerably from one subject discipline to another, and from person to person within the same discipline. What all research does have in common is the following processes:

1   Definition of the research question or hypothesis
2   Data collection
3   Data analysis
4   Interpretation of findings
5   Presentation and dissemination of the results

Who can do research?

You can! With the right guidance and preparation you can carry out research in your chosen field. Most researchers feel overwhelmed from time to time with the task they have (or someone else has) set, but if you follow tried and tested procedures and sit back and take stock from time to time you will get there in the end. The main reason that research is abandoned is that the researcher has not thoroughly checked out the feasibility of the project. (We will look at this in more detail later in this chapter.) However, sometimes circumstances outside of our control do change – so much so that what looked feasible at the start can turn out not to be so. In such cases (which are thankfully rare) there is no alternative but to pick yourself up and try another route. Such a scenario is simply part of 'doing research' which by definition is doing something that is unknown and not entirely predictable. In other words, research is risky.

Why do research?

All researchers have a different combination of motivations for doing research. Yours will almost certainly include the desire to obtain the qualification / accreditation for the course of which your current or anticipated research project is a part. However, your choice of a particular subject area / topic will almost certainly include other motivations as well. It is important to be able to recognise what your motivations are, not least because they will almost certainly affect your choice of topic and how you conduct your research. They could even affect the outcome of your research.

Activity Twenty-Five

Make a list of what *your* motivations are. (You may find, if you don't have any, that it would be better to return to this activity once you have selected your topic.)

Note your response

Commentary

Some researchers consider that they are totally detached from the project with which they are working, and are quite capable of remaining totally objective in carrying out every aspect of it, including writing up the results. Others know at the outset that they are going to become totally engrossed in the project. Those in the latter group invariably have much stronger motivation for the research and therefore much greater determination to succeed. Most of us fall somewhere in between.

All of us come to research with some life experience. Some of us conduct research directly as a result of some of that experience, be it good or bad. We may have something that we want to prove. This is not necessarily a bad thing, unless of course we let our desire to arrive at the 'right' conclusion cloud our judgement about how we conduct the research and thus the validity of it.

Some people do research because they need proof before they can get something done, for example to convince the fund-holder to pay for a project when the need has been conclusively determined. Others are involved in doing research that is related to their employment or place of work.

Doing research is the best way to learn how to do research. Many researchers, having written their report or dissertation, comment that only then do they feel fully competent to do the research. Needless to say – the more you do, the better you get at it.

What is 'good' research?

A debate exists about what constitutes 'good' research. Opinion is roughly divided along pure science versus social science lines, or pure versus applied research. Whatever type of research you ultimately choose to do, that research must be academically rigorous. Exactly what constitutes academic rigour in your subject discipline will become apparent as you progress with your programme of study, but essentially it involves substantiating your arguments with evidence.

Approaches to research

Much is written about research methodology. 'Methodology' literally means the study or science of method. Within the context of conducting research it means rather more than this. It refers, not simply to a list of different research methods that you employ to collect and analyse data, but rather to the overall approach that you take to conducting research. It is really a combination of the principles or perspectives behind the research, and the appropriate practical skills or tools required to conduct the research. For many researchers their approach to research is very much influenced by their ideology, which in turn both influences and is influenced by their views on *epistemology* (the study or theory of knowledge) and on *ontology* (theories about what exists or the study of being).

There is no one straightforward way of categorising research, and it is beyond the scope of this chapter to try and do so. But, crudely put, natural scientists traditionally have been seen as doing *pure* research, which is concerned with the creation of theories and the testing of those theories in laboratories, and social scientists have been the ones who have done *applied* research, testing theories in the real world. These approaches have also been known as 'positivist' and 'interpretive' and are largely concerned with the collection and analysis of quantitative and qualitative data respectively. Many researchers today find that a combination of the two broad approaches is more appropriate. Robson (2002) now refers to these approaches as needing 'fixed' or 'flexible' research designs or a combination of the two.

Within social science the debate still rages about whether, when essentially *people* are the subjects of the research, such research can be totally objective and therefore requiring a positivist approach, or whether subjectivity inevitably creeps in. There are also those that believe that no research, however 'scientific', can be totally objective. Some people would argue that it is possible to arrive at objective 'truth' and that research helps to establish and reinforce that truth. Such people may feel threatened with the idea that there can be several different perspectives to 'truth'.

May (2001: ch. 1: 7–27) and Robson (2002: ch. 2: 16–44) both provide an introduction to the major perspectives in social research. May (2001) explores the view that the methods and theories employed in the natural sciences are inapplicable to the social sciences since there are 'political and value considerations which affect our lives and are therefore a central part of our practice' (p. 8).

Robson (2002) explores what it means to be scientific and argues for its advantages, but goes on to consider the standard positivist view of science and rejects it as a basis for real world research. He also discusses relativist views and similarly rejects them. He goes on to review two main current approaches to social research: postpositivism and constructivism; considers a realist approach; and concludes that 'critical realism' is now an appropriate approach for real world research.

There is also a keen interest within the social sciences in the approach known as 'grounded theory' where explanation and theory are fashioned directly from the analysis of data, rather than the research starting out with a theory or hypothesis. This is based on the qualitative research of Glaser and Strauss (1967).

You may consider that such theoretical considerations are secondary to the actual doing of research. If you are studying and researching in a scientific discipline then you will probably find less discussion of these issues. However, such principles form the foundation of any social research and must be understood before moving on to other considerations, such as choice of methods. When doing further reading about approaches to research, try to relate the ideas to your own research ideas, as well as to your own inclinations, and try to decide which perspective or combination of perspectives best suits you and your research.

Methodological approaches

You will at some stage need to look at specific types of methodology which are available for you to choose from. Some approaches or strategies are those described as:

- Experimental research
- Survey research
- Qualitative research
- Quantitative research
- Comparative research
- Longitudinal research
- Documentary research
- Action research
- Evaluation research
- Case study research
- Ethnography (study of groups or communities)
- Feminist methodology
- Grounded theory research

The above categories are not mutually exclusive, indeed some involve the use of others. For instance: ethnography is regarded by some (but not all) as a type of qualitative research and may use a case study approach; comparative research may use survey research; and action research may be quantitative.

Several books listed in the Further Resources and References provide a detailed description of different methodologies. For example, Robson (2002: ch. 4) explores the question of research design by developing a framework for design that links purpose, theory, research questions, methods and sampling strategy. He considers fixed (experimental and non-experimental), flexible and multiple research strategies. In particular he looks at the three flexible strategies of case studies, ethnographic studies and grounded theory studies. He provides a clear and useful guide to selecting the most appropriate strategy for your project, and illustrates the section with several examples. Having looked at the question of research strategy using this broad approach, Robson then devotes the following three chapters to looking in detail at design: in Chapters 5 and 6 there is a more detailed discussion of fixed and flexible designs, concentrating on design issues specific to each strategy; and in Chapter 7 evaluation research and action research are discussed.

In addition to Robson (2002), you will find relevant chapters in May (2001). For instance: Chapter 7 on participant observation (an alternative term for ethnography); Chapter 8 on documentary research in social research; and Chapter 9 on comparative research. Documentary research is covered in more detail in Sapsford and Jupp (1996: ch. 6). Action research is dealt with in detail by Robson (2002: ch. 7, pp. 215–19 and Appendix B). The last two references are taking you into a great deal of detail about methods for conducting research.

Your project proposal

At some stage, you will need to write a project proposal. Essentially this will state not only *what* it is you are going to research, but also *why* you have chosen this particular topic, *how* you are going to go about conducting the research, within what *time-scale* and with what *resources*, and how you are going to *analyse the findings*.

Choosing the topic

Some of you reading this book may already have quite definite ideas about what the subject of your research project will be. Others (probably the majority) will not. Some of you in the latter category will, however, know the broad subject area in which you want to work. The task before you is to narrow down that broad area to a fairly narrow topic for consideration. If you are reading this book at the beginning of a two- or three-year course you may feel that you have plenty of time to consider this – after all the dissertation is the final piece of coursework to be submitted. In fact it is important to try and decide on your topic at quite an early stage. The practicalities of obtaining resources or collecting data can sometimes take months, so the sooner you begin to plan the project the better. That doesn't mean to say that you will know what the title of your dissertation is going to be. For most people the final version of the title is decided upon at the last minute, having been through many variations along the way. Most people arrive at their exact choice of topic after a considerable amount of reading and discussion with other students / colleagues at work / their supervisors.

Activity Twenty-Six

For now make a note of the topic you have in mind at the moment. Don't worry too much if it is still a fairly broad topic, there will be opportunity to narrow it down later, especially as you conduct your literature search.

Note your response

8.2 Literature searching and reviewing

Anyone beginning research needs to carry out comprehensive literature searching and reviewing for the following reasons:

- To discover what research already exists in the broad subject field
- To rule out the possibility of someone having already done the same research
- To help you decide upon the exact nature of your research
- To increase your knowledge and understanding in the subject field

This book cannot possibly give a detailed guide to literature searching in every field. What it can do, however, is to indicate in general terms the sort of searching tools that are available in most libraries, especially in academic libraries. What you *must* do is go to the library that will be your main resource centre and collect from there the various guides on literature searching that the library produces. If these do not appear to be available at the main service counter ask to speak to the librarian in your subject area. S/he will be able to give you more specific help. Also, your fellow students / colleagues / supervisor should be able to guide you.

In seeking literature relevant to your field you are searching for very specific data from a huge amount of data. Those data are stored in a number of bibliographical databases, which are collections of data. Bibliographical databases are databanks that provide information about specific items of literature. Within the context of literature searching, databases can be divided into a number of different categories, which are explained below. Some are produced in paper format and others are available in electronic format and can be accessed using a computer, either from a CD-ROM or via an online service. You should be able to find details of books, journal articles, conference proceedings and dissertations using the various tools that are available.

You were introduced in Chapter 6 to ways of finding relevant resources for your assignments. Whilst you may need to go into greater depth of searching for resources for your research project, the basic tools for doing so are essentially the same. In addition to those listed in Chapter 6, you will find the following resources particularly useful when doing your research project.

Current research

It is important to try to establish what research is currently being conducted in the same general subject field as your own. This is actually very difficult to do. One way is to try and attend relevant conferences and talk to people making presentations who will know what is happening in the field. Another is to consult various indexes of current research.

There are indexes for particular subject areas, such as *EUDISED* (*European Educational Research Yearbook*), published in printed format annually by the Council of Europe, or the *Register of Educational Research in the UK*, published by the National Foundation of

Educational Research (NFER) in England and Wales. This database is available as a series of bound printed volumes as well as being held electronically on a computer at the NFER. It seeks to include all recently completed and ongoing research in the UK in education and related fields. For a nominal charge, staff at NFER will conduct searches on the electronic database. They accept requests by phone, letter or email (enquiries@nfer.ac.uk).

For details of Economic and Social Research Council (ESRC) research awards and the publications and research activities which are the product of these awards you can use *REGARD* a recently introduced database service containing a wide range of information on social science research. It is accessible via their website at: http://www.regard.ac.uk/regard/about/index_html

You could also look at the websites of other big funding bodies and research centres in your subject area, for example: Centre for Research in Public Sector Management at: http://www.canberra.edu.au/management/crpsm/welcome.htm and Joseph Rowntree Foundation at: http://www.jrf.org.uk/

Most libraries will have a number of other compilations of research published in various subject fields by different bodies / publishing houses. Unfortunately, by the time they are published they are already out of date, but if you want to see what has been researched in the recent past they are a useful source. Search your library's catalogue for details.

For those working in the scientific and technological fields you can use patents information to help avoid duplicating existing research and development work. A huge amount of patents information is now available for free on the web. For example, the IBM Intellectual Property Network (now run by Delphion) covers patents from the United States, Europe and Japan from 1974 to date. Most of these patents documents are freely available on the website, or can be purchased online for a small fee. For older patents material and a more thorough search of worldwide patents literature you can visit one of the 14 Patents Information Network units (PIN units) around the country for a free consultation. The Leeds PIN unit is the second largest after London's and holds 24 million documents from 16 countries. Take a look at their website within the libraries pages of the Leeds City Council site at http://www.leeds.gov.uk/ for opening hours and contact details. There are also PIN units in the public libraries of other large cities and towns around the country from Aberdeen to Plymouth. See the patents website at http://www.bl.uk/patents for details.

Grey literature

Unpublished papers about current research are one form of so-called 'grey literature' which is very hard to trace. An initiative developed at the British Education Index (BEI) Office, University of Leeds, is the Education-line Project (http://www.leeds.ac.uk/educol/). The primary purpose of Education-line is to establish and maintain a database of pre-print and grey literature in education and training, providing a forum for discussion and facilitating early access to significant unpublished and pre-published research. The database contains reports, conference papers, working papers and so on.

NetEc (http://netec.mcc.ac.uk/NetEc.html) is a database of economics working papers, many of which are freely available in full text.

The *Physics Pre-Print Archive* (http://xxx.soton.ac.uk/) is one of a number of fully automated electronic archive and distribution servers for research papers prior to publication in the subject areas of physics, mathematics, nonlinear sciences, computational linguistics and neuroscience. The archives are available either on the web or by email. You can view abstracts of papers and download (or receive by email) the full papers. Users can also register to automatically receive a listing of newly submitted papers in areas of interest to them when papers are received in those areas. These listings are sent by email.

The *GrayLIT Network* (http://www.osti.gov/graylit/) 'makes the gray literature of US Federal Agencies easily available over the Internet. It taps into the search engines of distributed gray literature collections, enabling the user to find information without first having to know the sponsoring agency.'

Theses and dissertations

To discover what research has recently been completed you will need to consult an index to theses / dissertations. Your library may well hold a separate index to the theses / dissertations that it has in its own stock. There are also various published indexes to theses / dissertations. Details of these will be available in your library. For example:

Dissertation Abstracts lists doctoral dissertations (theses) in all subject disciplines and covers USA, Canada and some European countries (some British universities are not covered). The electronic version of this database covers 1861 onwards. It is called *Digital Dissertations* and can be found at: http://wwwlib.umi.com/dissertations/search/ The electronic version of *Index to Theses* at http://www.theses.com/ currently covers UK and Irish theses accepted from 1970 to 2001. The printed version takes coverage back to 1950.

Activity Twenty-Seven

The literature search and review. This task once begun will be ongoing and it would be unwise to concentrate solely on this and not continue working your way through the rest of this book or your other study materials. However, it is crucial that you make a start on this process at an early stage in your studies. (*If you know that you have access to the Internet and will be searching for information on the World Wide Web you might be better working through the next section first and returning to this Activity later.*)

You may already have made an initial visit to the library that will be your main or sole resource centre to discover what information sources are available (see Activity Nineteen). If you haven't you would be well advised to do so sooner rather than later. When you make that visit you need to make a note of those sources of information likely to be most relevant to your field of study.

Once you have some ideas for your research topic, and indeed for other assignments in your programme of study, and you have identified the sources, you need to begin to carry out searches systematically in order to discover what is available in your field. Make sure that you keep careful notes of the search strategy, the sources searched and of those items that the searches produce. You may want to input notes directly into your computer, thus beginning what eventually will become your bibliography. There is now software available to help you do this (see below). Even without such software, it is recommended that you download the results of any electronic searches to a floppy disk in text format. You will then have an accurate record of the search together with the search terms used.

Using 5 × 3 inch (c. 13 × 8 cm) cards, whilst still an excellent low-tech (and extremely portable) way of storing bibliographical information, does carry with it the potential for error. Great care needs to be taken in noting down accurately the bibliographical information. Don't forget to note the source of information for each item. It could save you hours trying to track down this information at some future date when you discover, for instance, that you don't have the volume number for a journal article.

Once you have located the items identified as potentially relevant and begin to read them, make notes about them, their usefulness, point of view, conclusions and so on. This will form the basis of your literature review when you write up your dissertation / research report and in the intervening time act as a very useful annotated bibliography.

A specific time cannot be set for this task – it will take you several hours, days – even weeks. Even after you have started to conduct your own research you need to continue to keep up with what else is happening in the field.

Personal bibliographic software

There are packages now available for helping researchers keep track of their references. These allow you to create and organise a database of references imported from bibliographic databases (*Web of Science*, and so on), other database packages (*Access, Idealist*) or those entered by hand. They automatically create in-text citations and bibliographies in your word processor in your chosen style. Examples of such packages are *Endnote* and *Reference Manager* both available from Citewise.com (http://www.citewise.com/). You may find that one or the other is available on the PCs in the computer clusters of some universities or colleges.

Modern information technologies can provide, not only access to literature in your field and assist in bibliographical referencing, but also can help you to conduct the research itself. The following section looks at such possibilities in detail.

8.3 Using the World Wide Web for research

The web is full of useful information to help you when doing research. Unfortunately it also has rather a lot of totally irrelevant information. It is very easy to fall into the trap of thinking that spending hours 'surfing the net' is the equivalent of doing research. It is probably advisable to set yourself limits on the amount of time you spend searching and *stick to them!* In order to spend your time most effectively you are best avoiding searching the web at busy times of the day *and* you need to make use of the growing number of 'tools' which are now available to help you search for relevant material.

The best starting point for using the web for research is almost certainly the website that is maintained by the college or university where you are registered for your course. In most cases the library or resource centre will provide a 'gateway' from its own website to many other useful resources.

The tools you are likely to find most useful for the purposes of research fall into three broad categories: search engines, subject portals and bibliographical databases. The first two will lead you to information on websites, the third may lead you (indirectly) to journal articles that are available on the web, but will primarily provide bibliographical information and possibly abstracts about articles, which you will then need to obtain in paper format.

Information on the web is changing constantly and therefore dates very quickly. You will need to discover new sources for yourself in the future, but for the present the information provided below should prove useful. Whichever tools you are going to use to search the web, it is crucial that you first develop your search strategy – planning your search carefully will mean that you retrieve the material that suits your purpose more quickly. If you do not achieve the results you would like, you will need to look at your search results to see if they indicate how you can modify your initial search. Searching the web may yield full text documents, but often you will be retrieving references to other sources, often in paper format, which you will then need to trace using your library catalogue.

Search strategies

In planning any search there are a number of steps to take:

1 Define your topic, that is establish its scope and the keywords for searching.
2 Structure your search.
3 Choose appropriate information sources to search (see Search engines, Subject portals, and Bibliographical databases below).
4 Perform your search.
5 View the results.
6 Review your results and refine the search if necessary.

If you don't find the information you need at first you may need to go back and revisit some of the steps.

Define your topic: scope and keywords

Think carefully about the sorts of words you could use to describe your topic effectively. Thoughtstorm the topic, so that you write down as many keywords as you can think of that describe it. Use both broad terms and more specific ones, so that you can decide if you want to focus on a particular aspect of the topic. The narrower terms might also be useful if your first search finds too much information, or information that is too general for your needs.

Think also about the time period in which you are interested. Do you want current information or information that describes what has gone on in the past? Also relevant is the geographical context of your search. Are you interested in the UK aspects of a particular topic, or are international perspectives of interest to you?

Structure your search

Once you have a set of keywords you need to think about how you are going to use them to formulate a query in order to perform your search. Searches can be broadened or narrowed depending on how you combine your terms. The different tools you will use for searching databases on the web will each have a set way for you to combine your search terms.

Using 'AND', 'OR' and 'NOT'   For example, search terms can be combined using the operator AND, in order to narrow a search, or they can be combined using the operator OR, in order to broaden a search. However, different search tools will express the concepts AND and OR using different symbols. Some may use the words, others a comma for

OR, or a plus sign for AND. On screen help is always available for you to check how to express these operators.

The operator NOT is sometimes available to exclude terms. For example, if you found that you were retrieving a lot of material on science education by searching for *mathematics AND secondary*, you could re-run the search explicitly excluding science (*mathematics AND secondary) NOT science*. Brackets are used to make sure that the sense of the query is clear where more than one operator is used.

Using truncation and wild cards   In some instances you may want to truncate your terms, to pick up singular and plural forms of a term, or you may want to allow for alternative spellings by inserting wildcard characters. Often truncation and wildcard characters are expressed using an asterisk, a question mark or a dollar symbol, depending on the search tool or database being used. For example, where an asterisk is used for truncation, *child** will pick up the terms *child, children* and *childhood* (as well as *childless*), and where a question mark is used as a wildcard, *organi?ation* will pick up *organisation* and *organization*.

Using phrases   Some search tools and databases allow you to search for specific phrases, often by enclosing the phrase in quotation marks, such as '*University of Leeds*'.

Searching fields   Field searching is a function which many search engines offer. Field searching enables you to search for a particular word or phrase in a specific field of a document (such as the title). It is likely that a document which has your chosen keyword in its title will be more relevant to your needs than one that simply mentions the word in passing somewhere in the body of the document. In *Alta Vista* (see below) you can search for a word in the title of documents by typing *title:* in front of the word, such as *title:technology*. Note that the keyword appears directly after the colon, with no spaces. The word *title* should be typed in lower case.

Perform your search

Only once you are satisfied that you have a good structure for your search and have selected the appropriate sources should you actually perform the search. Searching can be time consuming and if you are working from home it can also be very expensive on your phone bill if you are paying for an Internet connection.

View the search results

Once you have performed your search, take a look at your search results displayed on screen. Most search engines use a facility known as 'relevancy ranking' in order to rank your search results in 'best match' order, so that the documents that are most relevant to your keywords appear near the top of the list of your results. This means that the first page of results is likely to be more relevant to your needs than subsequent pages.

Review and refine your search

Once you have looked at your results, any flaws in your search strategy should become apparent. If you have retrieved an unmanageably large number of results, think about repeating your search using more specific terms, or incorporating more terms using AND. If you are finding very few relevant items, are there other terms you could use? Are you making full use of the tools available to you? If you are still not retrieving items, think about other sources you could search.

Search engines

These will search the whole of the web and give you a list of addresses of websites (URLs) where you will find information on a very specific subject. If you make your search terms too broad, a search could generate hundreds if not thousands of URLs. Some search engines are better than others for a particular subject area and there are those that are more appropriate to use for academic purposes, since they control the web pages that are included in their databases. There are also those that are easier to use than others because they have more flexible search query language and features such as phrase searching, Boolean searching and restricting the search by date. (Boolean searching is searching according to a set of rules about word order and use of symbols to aid the search.) *Alta Vista* and *Google* are two examples of search engines that incorporate many such features.

Some search engines are 'meta' search engines (for example *MetaCrawler* and *Ask Jeeves*) that search multiple engines simultaneously. Whilst this may save time, you may lose some control over your search if you cannot be as specific in your search terms. To save time, consider using UK search engines if you are resident in the UK as they will probably be less busy than the ones cited in the US and you will be searching in a smaller database. For instance you could try using *Yahoo UK and Ireland* or *Alta Vista UK* rather than the full American equivalents.

Whichever search engine you are using the following tips will prove useful:

- Plan your search beforehand.
- Read the Help pages of the search engine.
- Use the Advanced Search option.
- Use phrases.
- Search in the titles of web pages.
- Don't look beyond the first couple of pages of results.
- If it looks useful – bookmark it!

Activity Twenty-Eight

Access the *Alta Vista* search engine, either via your library website or direct at: http://www.altavista.com or http://www.altavista.co.uk

Click your mouse inside the search form and type some keywords that describe your topic of interest. Try to use several words and use uncommon words if possible. Then click on the Find button to start your search. Bookmark (that is add to your list of Favourites) any pages you come across which may be useful for future reference.

Tips for using *Alta Vista* are available via the Help prompt.

Subject portals

These are tools that will provide you with lists of descriptions of websites by subject. Subject portals will provide you with information on specific subject areas, such as *ADAM* for Art, Design, Architecture and Media, *Biz-Ed* for business and education, *OMNI* for medical information and *SOSIG* for the social sciences. If you discover one for your subject area, bookmark it and always try it first. You are likely to find much higher quality materials for academic study (although less of it) using a subject portal than you will with a search engine, since portals have the advantage of having been reviewed by experts in the field.

Some subject portals provide information in much broader subject areas, e.g. *NISS* (National Information Services and Systems) and the *BUBL LINK* (Libraries of Networked Knowledge). *BUBL LINK* is the name of a catalogue of selected Internet resources covering all academic subject areas and catalogued according to the Dewey Decimal Classification (DDC). All items are selected, evaluated, catalogued and described. Links are checked and fixed each month. The current catalogue holds over 10,000 resources. Although this is much smaller than the databases of some major search engines, it can provide a more effective route to information for many subjects across all disciplines.

You can usually go from subject portals to the specific websites by clicking on the appropriate links on screen.

Activity Twenty-Nine

1   Access the *BUBL LINK*, either via your library website or direct at: http://www.bubl.ac.uk/link/
    Scroll down the list of subjects using the scroll bar on the right of the screen until you come to a subject that is of interest to you. Have a look at the range of resources available for your subject area by clicking on the appropriate links on screen. Bookmark any resources you come across that may be useful for future reference.

2   Explore the list of subject portals that are available on your library website.
    Choose a service that is relevant to your subject area and explore the resources it contains by searching or browsing. Bookmark any resources that may be useful for future reference.

Bibliographic databases on the web

Bibliographic databases giving references to the published literature in a specific subject area are a good way of identifying respected work in a subject area. There are numerous sources of bibliographical information on the web. These range from the very broad-based ones such as the *Eureka** Database Service and *Cambridge Scientific Abstracts** to more subject-specific databases such as *MEDLINE* for medical bibliographical data and *UKOP Online* for information on UK Official Publications.

Most databases (for example, those asterisked above) require a password to access them. In some cases this will be an *Athens* password, but in other cases it may be a password just for that one database or journal. For full details please follow the Information or Help links from your library catalogue record.

In addition, the *Web of Science* Database Service is divided by subject: arts and humanities / science / social science. On the whole, bibliographic databases provide only the information about, for example, a journal article, which you the user then have to locate for yourself. However, some databases now provide links to the full text of the documents themselves. (For further information on bibliographic databases see Section 6.6 on Abstracts, indexes and electronic databases.)

Electronic journals

A rapidly increasing number of academic journals are available on the web. Not all of these will be available to users of all libraries, since the individual library must pay a subscription before their users are allowed access. The library will provide a listing of the journals to which it subscribes, and links from its own website to those journals. Electronic journals should be listed in the library catalogue.

In addition to a library's own list, there are various other listings of electronic journals, for example, *Science Direct* and *Ingenta Journals*. It is often possible to obtain articles via such listings even when your own library does not have a subscription to the journal, but you will have to pay a fee yourself to, for example, *Ingenta Journals* (which currently has over 750,000 full text electronic articles available from an expanding range of more than 500 leading academic journals). The *BUBL Electronic Journals List* includes details of electronic newsletters and magazines of general interest produced within the UK higher education community.

Off-campus access to electronic resources

The majority of a library's electronic resources are likely to be available off-campus. Most of the web-based databases and electronic journals require a password for access. These passwords are kept on secure library web pages that cannot normally be viewed off-campus. However, there should be a way of remotely accessing the computer network of the institution at which you are registered as a student and find the password that is needed for access to the resources.

Current awareness services for bibliographical resources

It is potentially very time consuming to have to keep going back to the databases and running searches in order to keep up-to-date with new publications and developments in your field, although some databases (for example *MEDLINE*) allow you to store search strategies to re-run at a later date. Automated alerting services can take away some of the effort of scanning and browsing journals, bulletins, newsletters and websites, by doing this for you and sending you updates on new developments in your subject. There are a number of such services available.

The *Zetoc Service* (http://zetoc.mimas.ac.uk) from the British Library is a freely available automated alerting service that emails information about new publications direct to your mailbox. *Zetoc* covers over 20,000 journals and over 70,000 conference papers, with over 14 million articles in the database in total. You can receive:

- Electronic tables of contents from your favourite journals
- The results of regular searches on current journal and conference literature on any subject of your choice

Copies of all of the articles and conference papers in the database are available *at a charge* from the British Library, and can be ordered direct or through the document supply service in your library.

Elsevier Contents Direct (http://contentsdirect.elsevier.com/) is a current awareness service for publications from the major academic publisher, Elsevier. It enables you to save a list of journal titles for which you would like automatic notification of the latest tables of contents. You can also ask to be notified when new books in your subject area are published by Elsevier. The notification is sent to you by email whenever the database is updated and new books or journal issues are added. You also may be able to access the service via your library website.

Scholarly Articles Research Alerting (SARA) is run by the Taylor & Francis publishing group. It provides a service whereby you can register to regularly receive by email the contents pages of individual journals or clusters of journals which they publish in your subject field. They have a wide range of titles in the following subject areas: education, gender, healthcare and biomedicine, law, management, science and technology, social sciences and humanities. You will find their website at: http://www.tandf.co.uk/sara/

British Official Publications Current Awareness Service (BOPCAS) provides a free email alerting service whereby users can subscribe to one or more policy awareness lists and receive details of recent UK Official Publications on a weekly basis. Lists include: defence, economy, education, environment, Europe, health, law, science and technology, transport and welfare (accessible from: http://www.bopcas.com/).

Activity Thirty

Explore (briefly) the list of bibliographical databases that are available from your library's website. Bookmark those that are likely to be most useful when conducting your full-scale literature search.

Electronic networking

You can keep in touch with other people in your subject area via newsgroups and mailing lists on the Internet but, be warned, you can waste a lot of time reading messages posted to such groups and lists when the information is very peripheral to your research. You would be advised to be very selective in the groups and lists that you join. For more details about mailing lists see Section 3.5.

Newsgroups

A newsgroup is a discussion area on the Internet. Newsgroups are a public area (a bit like a notice board) where people can post information on a variety of topics and discuss their interests with other people. Newsgroups are organised into subjects. They are also organised by type, for example news, rec (recreation), soc (society), sci (science), comp (computers) and so forth (there are many more). Users can post to existing newsgroups, respond to previous posts, and create new newsgroups. You can use a service called *Google groups* to search the recent archives of newsgroups or to post your own messages to newsgroups (see: http://groups.google.com/).

Professional communities

A growing number of professional groups maintain their own websites and databases of researchers and academics in their field. For example, the *Community of Science* lists experts and funding opportunities across all fields. You can search *Community of Science* to find a researcher doing work in a particular field.

ChemWeb.com is the website of the World Wide Club for the Chemical Community. The site includes: databases containing abstracts, chemical structures, patents, other websites and so on; a Worldwide Job Exchange; The *Alchemist* – ChemWeb's own magazine; and a conference diary for the latest events and conferences.

Current awareness service for web resources

The Scout Report is a guide to new web resources which is published weekly on the web or by email by the Internet Scout Project. You can use it to keep up-to-date with new web resources in your subject area. There are reports for three broad subject areas: science and engineering, social sciences and humanities, and business and economics. The home page of the Scout Project website is http://scout.wisc.edu/

Evaluating websites for quality

Anyone with access to an Internet server can set up their own web pages. This means that there is little control over the quality of material that appears. If the information you find on a website is going to have any legitimacy / authority / validity you need to ask, and be able to glean satisfactory answers to, the following questions:

1   *Can you find out who is the author of this website?* This could be an individual or a corporate author. Is this information clearly available? Is there an email address available at which you could contact the author?

2   *Is there any indication of the designation or authority of the author?* Can you establish their credentials (for example, are they a member of staff in a university department)? Is there evidence that their organisation supports the information on the web page, is there a copyright statement or is a disclaimer visible on the page?

3   *Can you establish the corporate owner of the information?* This could be, for example, a university or a commercial company. Can you establish this from the URL if it isn't immediately obvious on the page? For example: does the URL end with '.ac.uk' (a UK university), or '.edu' (a university in the US), or '.edu.au' (an Australian university)?

4   *What is your impression of the reliability of the information?* On what basis can you form this impression (for example, from prior knowledge of the subject area, from looking at the bibliography or linked information and so on)?

5   *How up-to-date is the information?* Is there a date when the document was last modified or updated?

6   *What do you think about the way in which the information is structured?* Is it easy to find your way around the website? How have graphics been used? Does the text follow basic rules of grammar, spelling and so on?

From the answers to the above questions you will be able to form an overall opinion about the quality of any site you visit.

Activity Thirty-One

Revisit a couple of the sites you bookmarked in Activity Twenty-Eight and ask the above questions of each one.

8.4 Values and ethical issues

Values

We all hold to a set of values (based largely on our beliefs and our experiences of life) and constantly make value judgements (often unconsciously). When doing research we must become increasingly aware of the values we hold and be conscious of how they might affect our work. In an in-depth analysis of values and ethics in the research process, Tim May (2001: 46–58) includes (amongst others) the following questions that all researchers must ask themselves:

- What are value judgements?
- How do values enter the research process?

May (2001: 51) identifies five stages at which values enter the research process:

1 Interests leading to research
2 Aims, objectives and design of research project
3 Data collection process
4 Interpretation of the data
5 The use made of the research findings

When you come to the stage of planning your research project you will need to consider how your own values may affect the research project *at each of the stages identified above*. You will need to identify what those values are and decide what steps it might be appropriate to take to minimise the effect. You may, of course, acknowledge your values, yet consider that you do not need to reduce their effect upon your research. This may be because you will be conducting research that positively benefits from those values or be working with people with whom you will collaborate and to whom you will declare those values.

Ethical issues

As Robson (2002: 65) points out: 'It is vital that, at a very early stage of your preparations to carry out an enquiry, you give serious thought to these ethical aspects of what you are proposing'. Broadly speaking, ethics refer to a set of principles or rules that affect or control our behaviour. We each tend to develop our own code of conduct by which we live our lives (usually within the context of a set of laws of the land in which we are resident), but in research, as in various other areas of our lives, that code of conduct will often be imposed on us. Often the ethical issues with which you must be concerned are imposed on you by a professional body, by your employer (if your research is to be done within your place of work), by your sponsor (often a government agency) or other funding body (for example ESRC), or by your research institution (such as the university where you are registered). There are no easy answers to the ethical questions that are raised in research.

Activity Thirty-Two

Read the *Ethical Principles for Conducting Research with Human Participants*, published by the British Psychological Society (BPS). This is available in a file to download from the BPS website (http://www.bps.org.uk/documents/code.pdf). It raises major issues that are applicable to many fields of investigation, for example consent, confidentiality and the giving of advice.

There is also a useful short summary of ethical issues at: http://trochim.human.cornell.edu/kb/ethics.htm – This is part of Bill Trochim's Knowledge Base at the online Centre for Social Research Methods at Cornell University, USA.

A detailed exploration of ethical issues as they relate to student researchers can also be found in *The Student's Guide to Research Ethics* by Paul Oliver (2003).

What ethical issues do you need to consider for your own project? Obtain your own copy of the ethical guidelines likely to be most relevant to your area of research. Your tutor should be able to provide you with other examples appropriate to your subject area from the British Sociological Association, the Socio-Legal Studies Association, the Medical Research Council and so on. Failing that, your academic department is likely to issue its own guide for students conducting research. Although the issues identified in the guidelines may not be identical to the ones that you may raise, you may find that the guidelines prompt you to think of similar issues that need to be considered.

Note your response

Activity Thirty-Three

What steps do you need to take to resolve each of the ethical dilemmas that have been raised by reading the guidelines?

Note your response

8.5 Feasibility

It is crucial that you are realistic about what can be achieved in the time-scale available for your project. Before committing yourself to your project and completing and submitting your research proposal, you should ask yourself the following questions about the feasibility of the research:

1   *Do I have the time?* What is the time-scale for the research? Is it possible to complete all the negotiation of access / data collection / data analysis / report writing that the project would involve? Be realistic.

2   *Do I have the money?* Do you have the money for travel and accommodation, during data collection away from your usual residence; preparation of questionnaires; cost of phone calls; analysis of data by external agents; stationery / equipment?

3   *Do I have access?* Do you have access to buildings / institutions / individuals / documents, within the time-scale available, to be able to collect the data you require? (Blaxter *et al.* (2001: 143–5) looks in some detail at how to gain access to data and offers some strategies to consider if access is refused.)

4   *Do I have the skills?* Do you have the keyboard skills, analytical skills? Do you have the required skills to do the research or the time to acquire them?

5   *Do I have the knowledge about the subject?* Do you have the required knowledge to do the research or the time to acquire it?

In all cases you need to identify in advance any potential problems and consider finding solutions or alternatives.

Robson (2002: 376–84) provides further advice on issues of feasibility, especially on negotiating access.

8.6 Evaluating other people's research projects

You can discover a lot about how to do research (and how *not* to do it) by looking at other people's research reports / dissertations. It will help you to further formulate your ideas about your own research.

Whenever you read a report (and indeed plan your own research and report), the following questions need to be considered:

1   Has the study been done before? (You will know the answer to this from your literature search and search of current / recent research.)
2   Does the study end up answering the question set at the beginning?
3   Are the conclusions justified by the results?
4   How do the results relate to the findings of others?
5   Do the findings fit to an existing or proposed model?
6   Could you repeat the study from the information given?
7   Do the authors set out the implications of their work for your subject area and for further research?

In addition, consider the following questions about the data collection and analysis:

1   Were the data collection methods suited to the subjects being researched and the question being addressed?
2   Are the results reliable?
3   Are the results valid?
4   Are the results generalisable?
5   Is there any bias?
6   Are the findings clearly presented?

Activity Thirty-Four

Critically evaluate two or three project reports / dissertations written about research carried out in your subject area. You should be able to obtain access to these in your local university library or (for reports of smaller research projects) in the department of the institution where you are registered as a student. Ask the above questions as you read the report and make a note of the answers.

In the light of your findings, make a note of issues that you need to consider more carefully about your own research before you begin it.

Note your response

8.7 Managing your research project

You need to think carefully about managing the project – planning ahead, managing your time, and keeping accurate records of any number of things. Don't always be in a hurry to do things. Time spent in reflection or contemplation is time well spent – provided, of course, the ideas that are generated are eventually translated into action!

Plan / do / review

Making plans is all very well but they are only of value if you have some way of reviewing where you have got to in your plan. It is a good idea, therefore, to make arrangements with your tutor(s) about who is going to monitor your progress and how this is to be done. Ideally it should be a joint effort, though the primary responsibility is yours. If you are the sort of person who values some external pressure to help you meet deadlines, you could perhaps ask your tutor(s) to build in regular monitoring sessions when they ask to discuss a piece of written work with you or a report you have written on your own review of your progress.

You will need to be realistic about the workload here – yours and theirs – and be clear about the purpose of each meeting. Don't be tempted to review too often: you need the time in between to get some real work done.

> 'The time given for the dissertation is in proportion to the length of the work but be aware it is a much more intense and complex experience.'
>
> 'Assignments / dissertations *always* take longer than anticipated.'

Managing your time

We looked in some detail in Section 4.6 at the question of time management for the duration of your whole period of study. At this point you need to pay particular attention to the time management issues of conducting your research project.

Research schedule

Bearing in mind the issues raised in Section 4.6 and your responses to the activities there, draw up a *realistic* and more detailed schedule for the whole of the research project. Remember that you need to allow plenty of time for data analysis and presentation (especially if you are transcribing and editing from tape recordings of meetings or interviews) and for the writing of the dissertation or research report. The preparation of tables and graphs (even using computer software) and the final editing of your report can be very time consuming. The deadline for finishing all of this is usually imposed by external factors, such as the submission date of your research report for your course of study or the date stated by your employer if you are planning work-related research. For some part-time programmes of study, course leaders may be happy for the dissertation or report to be submitted some time later than the official end of the period of study, well after other assignments and any formal written examinations have been completed. Be sure to check what the regulations are for your particular course (and institution) and also to enquire whether or not any additional fees will have to be paid if you extend the course in this way.

Using the submission date as your end date you can calculate how many months you have between now and then and design a work schedule. This might simply be a list of tasks with proposed completion dates against them, but in order to see the relationship between different tasks, including the rest of your studies, it is better to draw up some form of table or chart that is divided up into monthly, weekly or even daily sections on one axis and by a series of tasks on the other.

Although you may have included your research project and / or the writing of the dissertation in the earlier Gantt chart for your whole course, it is important to look in more detail at the research project and the tasks associated with it. One example of what a research schedule might look like is given in Figure 8.1.

> 'I was awarded a scholarship and a research grant in my second year, which I used to . . . cover my work one day a week for three months whilst I did my research.'

Month	1	2	3	4	5	6	7	8	9	10	11	12
Literature search and review	→	→	→									
Finish this book	→											
Plan own research	→	→										
Observe research of A. N. Other	→	→	→									
Conduct pilot tests				→								
Analyse and reflect on pilot tests					→							
Collect main data						→	→	→				
Analyse data								→	→			
Write dissertation										→	→	→

Figure 8.1   Research schedule

Activity Thirty-Five

Although you will not be able to fill in the 'tasks' in detail until you have decided upon the exact methods you are going to use, make a start on drafting your schedule. You could even include the reading of this book as one of the tasks. You could also make an entry for assisting on someone else's research or reading about other research and you could certainly include the literature search and review, which you may already have begun and which will be ongoing for a few more weeks yet. Clearly this and many other tasks will overlap and will therefore appear in the same week or month of the schedule. Other tasks will have to be completed consecutively rather than concurrently, since the commencement of one is dependent upon the completion of the other. The data collection needs to include time for the execution and analysis of the pilot and for reflection on these before scheduling the main data collection time. You also need to build in some allowance for a degree of slippage. For instance, you may have to modify your strategy in the light of the results of the pilot work. The new strategy will need to be piloted if there are more than just minor changes.

Commentary

Other suggestions for charting your time schedule, together with ideas for making the most of your time, are included in Orna (1995: ch. 5). As Orna points out (p. 82) you are often dependent on other people to be able to meet your deadlines so you need to plan well ahead and make your arrangements in good time. There is also a useful chapter in Cryer (2000: ch. 10) on managing yourself and your time.

Record-keeping

Every step along the way you need to keep good records. They might take the form of notes on sources of information – be they people, addresses, references to literature or whatever – or a detailed report on progress (or lack of it!). The largest amount of data will be that which is generated in the process of actually doing the research. In every respect it is crucial to organise your data. Your means of doing this may take various forms, for example:

- Diary of research
- Card indexes
- Loose-leaf files
- Computer files
- Audio and / or video tapes
- Notebook

Diary of research

A research diary could take different forms. For some people it can become a reflective journal, which serves a therapeutic purpose for the researcher as well as being a source of information / inspiration to return to at a later date. For others, although it may be reflective in some senses, it is kept very precisely for the purpose of building a record of the research process and forms the basis of various elements of the research report.

Whilst a research diary can clearly be beneficial for a number of different reasons it is probably more relevant for a research student or where the research project is large-scale. For a smaller project the amount of time actually needed to write the diary may be better spent doing other things. Alternatively the diary might be a very brief record of progress of the project, perhaps written on a weekly basis. This can help the researcher to appreciate where more headway is needed.

Other records

You may want to create your *bibliographical database* directly onto your computer. This is no bad thing, since you will gradually build up an essential element of your research report. However, for ease of reference – especially when out and about – nothing can beat the 5 × 3 inch (*c.* 13 × 8 cm) or 6 × 4 inch (*c.* 15 × 10 cm) index cards that you can buy from the stationers. They can also be used for a *database of people* you contact, possibly cross-referenced to another containing *details of organisations, companies,* and so on. (See Section 8.2 for details of personal bibliographic software.)

Once you start actually collecting the *substantive data,* which is the subject of your research, you will need to be particularly organised. How you write up the results of, for instance, meetings or interviews is a question of personal choice. Eventually you will want to include at least a summary, if not a verbatim record, of interviews in your report so they will end up on computer, but in the short-term (especially if you are out 'in the field' for several days) you will want to ensure you have an accurate record of what was said. If the interviews are recorded on tape (audio or video) there is less urgency to write them up, but if you are making hand-written notes initially these should be done as soon as possible after the interview.

Don't be tempted to think that the very clear memory you have of what was said by a particular interviewee will stay with you. Even after two or three interviews the details all get a bit hazy and who said what becomes a bit confused. Since you might want to be able to re-arrange the order of the information collected in this way you might be better writing on cards (for relatively brief interviews) or using a loose-leaf folder.

Although you might not want to embark upon writing the research report until well into the project you might consider keeping a file (either loose-leaf or on computer) containing headings and sub-headings for the various sections of what will ultimately be your report and add notes to this from time to time. Again the low-tech version is more mobile (unless we're talking lap-top or palm-top computers!) and you can use coloured dividers to mark the different sections and new sheets can easily be inserted.

At the very least, always have a notebook handy. You never know when those brilliant ideas are going to come to you. What seems glaringly obvious and abundantly clear at 3:00 am becomes a blur after a few more hours sleep.

Filing system

Whatever form your record-keeping takes, make sure that you have an efficient and effective filing system. In this way you will be able to locate the information you need when you need it. Classify the files you create in some way. On a computer you can do this by creating different sub-directories for documents covering the various components of your project. (Don't forget to have different floppy disks for your backup copies.) If you are creating paper files you could use different coloured folders for separate topics as well as labelling the folders clearly. Keep a record of the classifications you have used so that you don't create a new folder when one already exists. Make sure that you label the documents in some way so that you know which folder they belong in, maybe by simply marking the top of each with a coloured pen. Since each folder will contain several documents you might consider (especially for larger projects) using a simple card index system so that you know where each document is.

8.8 Reporting your findings

Writing your research report (or dissertation) is an integral and crucial part of the process of conducting research. The research has no real value unless what you find out is communicated to others. There are two stages to be considered here:

1   Writing-up the results and the conclusions you have drawn from those results
2   Disseminating those findings to others.

Both of these stages will be affected by your knowledge of who you want to read the findings and who needs / has a right to read them. It may be that different types of report will be needed to fulfil the different requirements. Whilst it may seem a long way off before you need to have your report(s) ready, it is never too soon to start thinking about what is going to go in it (them). (*You are likely to find much of what is included in this section on writing reports also relevant to writing your other assignments.*)

Your audience

Most of you reading this book will be registered for an accredited academic course and one of the requirements of that course will be to conduct research and produce a dissertation. Clearly your primary aim will be to meet the expectations of your tutor(s) and of the external examiners. Different departments within universities issue their own guides to writing a research report. The rules and regulations regarding length of report, whether or not and how it is bound, how many copies are needed, and so on will vary.

In addition, you may obtain some funding / sponsorship from an external body to help with the expenses incurred in conducting the research, or your employer may give you some form of grant. It is likely that someone somewhere will expect to be informed about the findings and that they will have their own expectations about how those findings will be presented.

Activity Thirty-Six

Before going any further, discover (or recover) information about who will require a report on your research and in what format that report is needed. Read this information and make brief notes.

Collect together into one folder any guidelines, documents, and so on that you come across which include such information. If details about the format of the report are included in a larger document, photocopy the relevant pages and keep them with other guidelines.

Note your response

Commentary

You need to have such guidelines constantly in mind when writing your report(s). It may be that if you have to write more than one report you can use some sections in both / all of them.

The content of the report

Whilst the exact format and final length of the report will vary according to the above factors, the basic outline will not. All that will change is the depth to which each aspect is analysed and the detail that is included. Essentially any research report will include the following:

- WHAT the research was.
- WHY the research was done.
- HOW the research was conducted.
- WHAT the results of the research are.
- HOW you have interpreted those results.
- WHERE you are going to go from here.

You can start to gather together notes for the first three sections from a very early stage, indeed the content of these sections will be needed for your research proposal. The most significant change for the final report will be that you will change to using the past tense! If you are restricted in the number of words you may use, make sure that every one counts. Don't go into detail about peripheral matters and don't try to cram everything in just because you've got it.

Writing the report

Just because *you* know your subject inside out by the time you have finished your research it doesn't mean to say that everyone else does. Even when it is going to be read by others in the same field, it is important to keep the style of your writing simple and clear. It doesn't make your work more worthy or intellectual because you use long, complicated sentences. The opposite is quite often the case. Where you do use jargon be sure to include a definition of the term in a glossary at the front or back of your report so that the uninitiated can check on meaning. It is especially important to remember this advice when writing a version of your report that will be read by a wider audience, say by first-year undergraduates reading your article in a journal.

Whilst there are conventions about most things to do with spelling, grammar, punctuation and abbreviations, there are many times when decisions are down to personal choice. (For instance, are you going to use full stops for 'e.g.', 'Dr', 'Mr' or 'USA'? Are you going to spell out 'seven' and 'nine' in full but use '11' and '46' in numbers?) In such instances make your mind up, note down your decision and stick to it. It is very irritating for all readers, but for examiners in particular, to see two or three different versions within the same document.

The ultimate aim of any writing is to enable the reader to grasp the meaning of what you are saying. This may be enhanced by the use of analogy and metaphor but don't set out to use them just for the sake of it. You may find that your reader won't be able to see the wood for the trees. Try to make your material straightforward and readable but interesting, so add a bit of variety. Gradually you will develop your own style that you will feel comfortable with. You might find it useful to ask a friend or helpful colleague to read some of your writing at a very early stage and to give constructive criticism of it. You will be less likely to be upset at this stage than asking someone to read your final draft when the deadline for submission is just two days away.

Citations and references

For an excellent guide to the technical aspects of writing reports (including the presentation of bibliographic information) see: Turabian (1982). For a more up-to-date British guide see *MHRA Style Guide: A Handbook for Authors, Editors, and Writers of Theses*, produced and published by the Modern Humanities Research Association (2002). The first chapter (on the preparation of copy) includes information on preparing copy on disk and on direct electronic submission. Other chapters provide the more traditional information on punctuation, references, footnotes, and so on. An electronic version of the guide is also available, downloadable in a PDF version for free, at: http://www.mhra.org.uk/Publications/Books/StyleGuide/index.html or by emailing mail@mhra.org.uk

Various online guides to citations and to the Harvard and other systems of referencing are available. Some of these may be available via your college or university library's website, but the following are two examples: *Cite Them Right – Guide to Organising Bibliographic References* is provided by Northumbria University (http://www.unn.ac.uk/central/isd/cite/). It covers both paper and electronic sources.

At http://www.staffs.ac.uk/services/library_and_info/cite2.html you will find a practical page outlining different citation systems including Harvard, numeric, MLA (Modern Languages Association) and APA (American Psychological Association) provided by Staffordshire University.

The references given throughout the main text and at the end of this book use the Harvard system, and so provide an example of that system.

Disseminating the findings

In addition to distributing copies of the report(s) to various people already on your list, you need to consider using other ways of disseminating the findings to a wider audience. One way is to go to conferences in your field and present papers. This has the added advantage that, if the papers are subsequently published, it also provides on opportunity for adding a publication to your CV. Another avenue (and one that you might consider before venturing out to the big conferences) is to hold a short seminar at which to deliver and discuss your findings. These are often held within various schools or departments of a university or at sessions organised by the various interdisciplinary research groups. The more you speak about your research in public, the more confident you will become (and the more familiar with the content!).

Getting published

It may be that in addition to submitting your dissertation for your diploma or degree your aim is to begin building up a list of publications. Whilst you can make enquiries at the outset about getting a monograph published, the slightly easier and less onerous task is perhaps to aim at getting an article or two in relevant academic journals. You are not likely to be paid for such an article but it will be a start. You have probably discovered (in the course of your own literature search) the sorts of journals that are likely to be interested in an article in your field. For ideas of other titles you can check the journals in your library and seek the advice of fellow students, colleagues and tutors. You will usually find guidelines within the current issue of a journal about how to submit your article for consideration. Take note of the suggestions on layout, length, referencing style and so on, or you may fall at the first hurdle. Your article is likely to be sent out to referees for scrutiny and may then come back to you with suggestions for improvement (which you may or may not be prepared to accept) so the whole process may take some time.

If you are already interested in finding out more about approaching a publisher about getting a book published, you might find it useful to read Ashcroft (1997: 121–7). If your work is within the broad field of educational research you will also find useful the annotated lists of education publishers and education journals provided in the same book, pp. 130–44. Sound advice is also provided in Luey (2002) and Thyer (1994).

Robson (2002) Chapter 15 includes a section on reporting on case studies and one on how to present recommendations in evaluation reports. There are also useful guidelines for revising the first draft of your report and some suggestions for further reading about reporting on the results of your enquiry. On p. 503 of Robson (2002) there are some samples of anti-sexist language from the BSA's *Guidelines on Anti-Sexist Language*.

Summary of Chapter 8

In this chapter you have:

- Begun your preparation for doing your research project by considering the nature of research and your approach to doing it
- Explored some of the numerous sources of bibliographical and other information that is available to assist you in that project, and begun to do your literature search
- Been alerted to the value and ethical issues that need to be considered when conducting research
- Considered the practicalities on managing your research project and reporting your findings

9 Course-specific information

Introduction

Most of the information that is specific to your course should be sent to you by the course administrator in the school or department of the college or university where you are registered for your course. Details may be included in various letters that are sent out to students or in a course handbook or student handbook that is distributed at the start of your studies. If you have received this guide to studying at a distance from the course administrator as part of an initial pack of materials, the chances are that you have already received other information as well. This chapter of the guide is provided to act as a *checklist* for you, so that you can identify if there is any information that you still need from the school / department. It is written in note form only. The notes are grouped together under various headings.

A note on registration and payment of fees

If you have registered for your course you will have already found your way through the maze that is your institution's registration procedure. If you have not yet registered, or are in the process of doing so, take heart – you will get there in the end.

Many traditional colleges and universities are still in a transitional period regarding the introduction of flexible procedures for the registration of distance learners and for the payment of fees, and the procedures at many institutions are still rather cumbersome. If you experience any difficulties in this area, my advice is always to contact the administrator of your specific course and they will intervene on your behalf.

9.1 Programme / course information

- Course website address
- Philosophy of the programme
- Course outline, including module dates
- Module outlines
- Other resources relevant to the whole course, such as text books / journals / websites / mailing lists
- Course materials you can expect to receive, and how and when you will receive them. (Detailed information about each module and resources specific to each module should be distributed a couple of weeks before the start of that module.)

Difficulty: 'No space between modules.'

'Course moves too quickly without any breathing space between modules.'

9.2 Contacts for support

Difficulty: 'Clarification re role of individual tutor and how much to access this support.'

- Role of and support you can expect from academic tutors / 'local' tutors / mentors / other students / course administrator / IT technicians / subject librarian.
- Contact details (name / phone and fax numbers / email address) of each of the above (note that the details of students should not be given out to other students unless express permission has been sought from the students to do this).
- How quickly can you expect a reply to a phone message or an

email? Is there a limit to the number of emails you can send or the number of minutes of phone calls you can make per module?
- Office location and hours.

> 'Email: essential for keeping in touch with tutors and other students. Email lists should be exchanged on 1st Study Day.'

9.3 Tutorial details

- Face to face / electronic?
- How many?
- When?
- Record of meetings?

9.4 Attendance requirements

- What are they?
- When are they?
- Residential / day schools? Are they compulsory? Penalties for non-attendance?

> 'Distance learning served me well – the day at the university once a month was a useful focus and made the best of our time there.'

Don't forget to inform the course administrator in advance if you know you will be absent from a face to face session because of a religious holiday or for any other reason. Similarly, if you find that you cannot attend a session or keep to any externally imposed schedule of work or submission of assignments because of illness (yours or that of a member of your family) make sure you contact the course administrator. In some circumstances you will need an official sickness certificate from your doctor.

9.5 Hardware / software requirements

These should be specified if there are elements of e-learning in your course (see Chapter 3 for more details on e-learning).

- Computer and Internet hardware, platform and specifications
- Software type and version
- Multimedia accessibility required

9.6 Electronic learner support

- Available via course website or virtual learning environment (VLE)?

9.7 Assessment specifications

Types of assessment

- Self, peer, tutor, formative, summative?
- What are they?
- Any choice?
- Forms of assessment – essays / posters / oral presentations / reports?

Submitting your work

- Where?
- When?
- How? Paper – in person / by post? Electronically – email attachments, web forms?
- Penalties for late submission?
- Details of how work should be presented – margin sizes / fonts / style of references.
- Is it possible to submit draft assignments for tutor comments before the final submission date?
- Will you be sent a reminder that your assignment is due?

Marking / assessment criteria?

- What are they?
- Is poor spelling or grammar penalised?
- Are there extra marks for good presentation?
- Is it possible to see assignments submitted by previous students?

Difficulty: 'Uncertainty over standard required.'

'Essay writing: a help would be to see samples of style expected (from previous groups).'

Feedback

- What form will the feedback take?
- How soon will that feedback be given?

9.8 Progress

- When / how often will my progress be monitored?
- Will review meetings be held?
- Are there self-assessment questions (SAQs) to monitor my own progress?

9.9 University / college information

- Information about university / college facilities and services, such as careers, welfare, library, students' union, and so on.
- Map of the university or college campus and of the department where you will go if you do have to attend face to face sessions.

A note on rules and regulations

Each institution has its own rules and regulations about attendance, missed deadlines for submission of assignments, non-attendance at examinations, and so on. Make sure that you are familiar with these at the start of your course. They should be available in your student handbook, which may be available in paper and / or web format.

And finally . . .

> 'Remember that you are a student of the university. You are entitled to use university and student union facilities. I found it important that the course staff sent us details of university activities.'
>
> 'Go to the graduation ceremony. You earn that day.'

Whilst the above suggestion about using the facilities at the university or college is clearly more relevant to students with relatively easy access to their institution, a lot of useful information for all students, including distance learners, is usually provided via the institution's website.

Summary of Chapter 9

> In this chapter you have:
>
> •   Checked the information you have previously received about your course and institution against this checklist
> •   Identified information you still need to obtain

Appendix
Understanding Learning

Types of education

The distinction has been made between two fundamental forms of education: *andragogy* and *pedagogy*. The terms were first used back in 1970 by Malcolm Knowles, though he later refined his views in 1980. Andragogy was defined as 'the art and science of helping adults learn' and pedagogy as 'the art and science of teaching children'. The distinction between adults and children has now largely been dropped, with the acceptance that children can learn by student-centred discovery methods and adults can learn by being taught by teachers. Knowles's ideas have been further developed by Jarvis (1985) and Jarvis *et al.* (1998) who likened pedagogy to 'education from above' and andragogy to 'education of equals'. It is probably fair to say that andragogy is more relevant to distance learning, although many distance learning courses will have some element of face to face teacher-centred 'taught' education.

Murdoch and Davies (1994) suggest that the defining feature of andragogy is that the learner is responsible for his or her own learning, that it is characterised by the student playing an active role in their learning, and that there will be a substantial element of self- and peer-assessment. All of these are certainly true of you as a distance learner.

Open, distance and flexible learning

There is much confusion over the terms 'distance learning', 'open learning' and 'flexible learning'. The confusion has arisen because there have been numerous definitions of these terms over the years. I offer the following definitions in the hope that they help to clear up any confusion.

Distance learning

Distance learning, as the word 'distance' implies, will usually take place remotely, usually at home or at work, although elements of it may take place on campus (for example, study days or tutorials). It is characterised by two key elements:

- Teacher and learner are separated but learning takes place under the auspices of an educational institution or organisation.
- Learning materials and two-way communication (rarely face to face) characterise the teaching and learning process.

Open learning

Open learning can take place on campus or remotely. It is learner-centred and the emphasis is on active learning. As with distance learning, learning materials are often used and it has traditionally been characterised by:

- Learners having more control (and flexibility) over the time, place and pace at which they learn.

Although learners in higher education may have *some* flexibility over time, place and pace of learning, the degree of flexibility is not usually significant due to the administrative constraints of registration, semesterisation and assessment. However, 'open learning' is the term often used to describe what might be better known as 'flexible learning'.

Further Resources

General study guides

Bourner, T. and Race, P. (1995) *How To Win as a Part-Time Student*, 2nd edn. London: Kogan Page.

Britton, A. and Cousins, A. (1998) *Study Skills: A Guide for Lifelong Learners*, rev. edn. London: Distance Learning Centre, South Bank University.

Buzan, T. (2000) *Use Your Head*, new edn. London: BBC Books.

Cottrell, S. (1999) *The Study Skills Handbook*. Basingstoke: Palgrave.

Drew, S. and Bingham, R. (2001) *The Student Skills Guide*, 2nd edn. Aldershot: Gower.

Ennis, E. and Keighren, J. (1997) *On Course: Preparing to Study by Distance Learning – A Short Guide*. Dundee: Distance Learning Section, Department of Orthopaedic and Trauma Surgery, University of Dundee.

Lashley, C. (1995) *Improving Study Skills: A Competence Approach*. New York: Cassell.

Lashley, C. and Best, W. (2001) *12 Steps to Study Success*. New York: Continuum International Publishing Group.

Lewis, R. (1997) *How to Manage Your Study Time*. Cambridge: National Extension College and Collins Educational.

Marshall, L. and Rowland, F. (1998) *A Guide to Learning Independently*, 3rd edn. Buckingham: Open University Press.

Northedge, A. (1990) *The Good Study Guide*. Milton Keynes: The Open University.

Powell, S. (1999) *Returning to Study: A Guide for Professionals*. Buckingham: Open University Press.

Race, P. (1996) *How to Win as an Open Learner: A Student's Guide to Tackling an Open Learning Course*, 2nd edn. Coventry: National Council for Educational Technology.

Rowntree, D. (1993) *Teach Yourself with Open Learning*, new edn. London: Kogan Page.

Rowntree, D. (1998) *Learn How to Study*, 4th edn. London: Warner.

Subject-specific study guides

Chambers, E. and Northedge, A. (1997) *The Arts Good Study Guide*. Milton Keynes: The Open University.

Giles, K. and Hedge, N. (eds) (1995) *The Manager's Good Study Guide*. Milton Keynes: The Open University.

The Language Learner's Good Study Guide. Milton Keynes: The Open University. (This book is only available direct from the Open University, not from bookshops.)

Northedge, A., Thomas, J., Lane, A. and Peasgood, A. (1997) *The Sciences Good Study Guide*. Milton Keynes: The Open University.

Guides to reading and writing

Collinson, D., Kirkup, G., Kyd, R. and Slocombe, L. (1992) *Plain English*, 2nd edn. Buckingham: Open University Press.

Creme P. and Lea, M.R. (2003) *Writing at University: A Guide for Students*, 2nd edn. Buckingham: Open University Press.

Fairbairn, G.J. and Fairbairn, S. (2001) *Reading at University*. Buckingham: Open University Press.

Fairbairn, G.J. and Winch, C. (1996) *Reading, Writing and Reasoning: A Guide for Students*, 2nd edn. Buckingham: Open University Press.

Hennessy, B. (2000) *Writing Successful Essays*. Plymouth: How to Books.

Hilton, C. and Hyder, M. (1992) *Getting to Grips with: Writing*. London: Letts Educational. (Covers basic grammar, punctuation and spelling and writing for specific purposes, e.g. a letter.)

Rose, J. (2001) *The Mature Student's Guide to Writing*. Basingstoke: Palgrave.

Woodward, K. (1991) *Open Teaching Toolkit: Reading and Note Taking*. Milton Keynes: The Open University.

Guides to sitting examinations

Acres, D. (1995) *How to Pass Exams Without Anxiety*, 4th edn. Plymouth: How to Books.

Orr, F. and Fletcher, C. (1998) *How to Pass Exams: And How to Prepare for Them With Less Anxiety*, 2nd edn. London: Allen & Unwin.

Tracy, E. (2002) *The Student's Guide to Exam Success*. Buckingham: Open University Press.

Guides to mathematics and statistics

Graham, A. (2001) *Basic Mathematics*, new edn. London: Hodder and Stoughton. (Teach Yourself Books)

Graham, L. and Sargent, D. (1981) *Countdown to Mathematics, Volumes 1 & 2*. Wokingham: Addison Wesley.

Owen, F. and Jones, R. (1994) *Statistics*, 4th ed. London: Pitman.

Rowntree, D. (1991) *Statistics Without Tears: A Primer for Non-Mathematicians*, new edn. London: Penguin.

Guide to science

Tennent, R.M. (ed.) (1971) *Science Data Book*. Edinburgh: Oliver and Boyd. (Basic scientific facts and figures.)

Guides to doing research

Bell, J. (1999) *Doing Your Research Project: A Guide for First-Time Researchers in Education and Social Science*, 3rd edn. Buckingham: Open University Press.

Blaikie, N. (1993) *Approaches to Social Enquiry*. Cambridge: Polity Press.

Bryman, A. and Burgess, R. G. (eds) (1994) *Analyzing Qualitative Data*. New York: Routledge. (Includes a chapter (8) on the use of computers.)

Bryman, A. and Cramer, D. (2001) *Quantitative Data Analysis with SPSS Release 10 for Windows: A Guide for Social Scientists*, updated edn. London, New York: Routledge.

Coffey, A. and Atkinson, P. (1996) *Making Sense of Qualitative Data: Complementary Research Strategies*. Thousand Oaks: Sage. (Includes a chapter (7) on computer-aided analysis.)

Cohen, L., Manion, L. and Morrison, K. (2000) *Research Methods in Education*, 5th rev. edn. London: Routledge.

Mason, J. (2002) *Qualitative Researching*, 2nd edn. Thousand Oaks: Sage.

Oppenheim, A.N. (1992) *Questionnaire Design, Interviewing and Attitude Measurement*. London: Printer Publishers.

Rubin, H. and Rubin, I.S. (1995) *Qualitative Interviewing: The Art of Hearing Data*. Thousand Oaks: Sage.

Study guides on the web

A number of universities in the UK have study skills and research skills guides on open access on the web: you could use a search engine such as Google to find these, or go via your library website. In particular, a growing number of university libraries provide a gateway to an ever-increasing number of good quality information skills materials on the web and other resources that support students. You may find that the information skills section on your library website provides brief abstracts of and links to websites on:

- Citations and references
- Database searching skills
- Finding good quality information on the Internet

A small selection of such resources are detailed below (and some on citations and referencing are provided in Chapter 8). Remember that the URLs to websites can change and you may need to find updated URLs by using a search engine.

- **Best Student Sites** is a website maintained at the University of Northumbria at Newcastle by Ian Winship and Alison McNab, the authors of *Student's Guide to the Internet* to complement and update their book. (It can be found at: http://www.unn.ac.uk/~iniw2/bestsite.htm) 'The Web sites in these pages are the most useful for UK students for academic purposes in terms of communication and information sources. Some are of general use; some illustrate types of Internet resources, while others are collections and directories to use to find the information you need' (Winship and McNab, Best Student Sites).
- **Bill Trochim's Centre for Social Research Methods.** http://trochim.human.cornell.edu/ (accessed 27 April 2003).
- **Honey and Mumford Learning Styles Questionnaire (LSQ).** Knowing about different learning styles and discovering what your preferred styles are can help you become a

more effective learner. The Honey and Mumford LSQ can be accessed online for a fee (£10 as of April 2003) at: http://www.peterhoney.com/main/

- **The RDN Virtual Training Suite** at http://www.vts.rdn.ac.uk/ provides a set of online tutorials in various subjects to help students, lecturers and researchers improve their information skills for the Internet environment. You can work at your own pace – there is no one monitoring you! The tutorials take around an hour each to complete, and include quizzes and interactive exercises to lighten the learning experience. Learning how to use the Internet more effectively can help you with your coursework, literature searching and research.

- **Study Guides and Strategies** at: http://www.iss.stthomas.edu/studyguides/was created by Joe Landsberger of Academic Web Services at the University of St Thomas, in St Paul, Minnesota, USA. It is collaboratively maintained across institutional and national boundaries and regularly revised. The site covers guides to learning and studying in general (including a section on *Succeeding in distance education courses*) as well as specific guides to learning with others, reading, writing and preparing for and taking tests. There are versions of the site available in many different languages.

- **VARK: A Resource Pack for Students and Teachers to Enhance Learning** (1998). The following website has been developed from where it is possible to take the VARK Questionnaire interactively: http://www.vark-learn.com/english/index.asp – Copyright is held by Neil D. Fleming, New Zealand, and Charles C. Bonwell, USA. This material may be used for staff or student development if attribution is given. It may not be published in paper or electronic form without the consent of the authors.

  From the website you can also buy copies of Fleming, N.D. and Bonwell, C.C. (2001) *How Do I Learn Best? A Student's Guide to Improved Learning.* (Published by the authors in New Zealand.)

References

Ashcroft, K. (1997) Getting published, in Jones, M., Siraj-Blatchford, J. and Ashcroft, K. *Researching into Student Learning and Support*. London: Kogan Page.

Blaxter, L., Hughes, C. and Tight, M. (2001) *How to Research*, 2nd edn. Buckingham: Open University Press.

Bloom, B.S., Engelhart, M.D., Furst, E.J., Hill, W.H. and Krathwohl, D.R. (eds) (1956) *Taxonomy of Educational Objectives: Handbook 1 – The Cognitive Domain*. London: Longman.

Cottrell, S. (1999) *The Study Skills Handbook*. Basingstoke: Palgrave.

Creme, P. and Lea, M.R. (2003) *Writing at University: A Guide for Students* 2nd edn. Buckingham: Open University Press.

Cryer, P. (2000) *The Research Student's Guide to Success*, 2nd edn. Buckingham: Open University Press.

Entwistle, N. and Ramsden, P. (1983) *Understanding Student Learning*. London: Croom Helm.

Fleming, N.D. and Bonwell, C.C. (2001) *How Do I Learn Best? A Student's Guide to Improved Learning*. (See Further Resources, Study guides on the web for more information.)

Glaser, B.G. and Strauss, A.L. (1967) *The Discovery of Grounded Theory*. Chicago: Aldine.

Honey, P. and Mumford, A. ([1982] 1992) *The Manual of Learning Styles*, 3rd edn. Maidenhead: Peter Honey (Both the 2nd and 3rd editions include a revised questionnaire. The questionnaire is also available on disk.)

Honey, P. and Mumford, A. (1995) *Using Your Learning Styles,* 3rd edn. Maidenhead: Peter Honey.

Jarvis, P. (1985) *The Sociology of Adult and Continuing Education*. London: Croom Helm.

Jarvis, P., Holford, J. and Griffin, C. (1998) *The Theory and Practice of Learning*. London: Kogan Page.

Knowles, M.S. (1970) *The Modern Practice of Adult Education: Andragogy vs Pedagogy* New York: Association Press.

Knowles, M.S. (1980) *The Modern Practice of Adult Education*, 2nd edn. Chicago: Association Press.

Kolb, D.A. (1984) *Experiential Learning: Experience as the Source of Learning and Development.* Englewood Cliffs, N.J.: Prentice Hall.

Luey, B. (2002) *Handbook for Academic Authors,* 4th edn. Cambridge: Cambridge University Press.

Marton, F. and Saljö, R. (1976) On qualitative differences in learning: I – outcome and process, *British Journal of Educational Psychology,* 46: 4–11.

May, T. (2001) *Social Research: Issues, Methods and Process,* 3rd edn. Buckingham: Open University Press.

Modern Humanities Research Association (MHRA) (2002) *MHRA Style Guide: A Handbook for Authors, Editors, and Writers of Theses.* London: MHRA.

Murdoch, A. and Davies, B. (1994) *An Introduction to Self-Directed Study.* London: Scutari Press.

Oliver, P. (2003) *The Student's Guide to Research Ethics.* Buckingham: Open University Press.

Orna, E. with Stevens, G. (1995) *Managing Information for Research.* Buckingham: Open University Press.

Phillips, E.M. and Pugh, D.S. (2000) *How to Get a PhD: A Handbook for Students and their Supervisors,* 3rd edn. Buckingham: Open University Press.

Philpot, M. (1997) Distance learning, *Educational Courses in Britain,* 18(6). (The author is Secretary of The Open and Distance Learning Quality Council, 27 Marylebone Road, London NW1 5JS.)

Rawlins, K. (1996) *Study Skills for Adult Learners.* London: Macmillan Magazines.

Robson, C. (2002) *Real World Research: A Resource for Social Scientists and Practitioner-Researchers,* 2nd edn. Oxford: Blackwell.

Rose, J. (2001) *The Mature Student's Guide to Writing.* Basingstoke: Palgrave.

Sapsford R. and Jupp, V. (eds) (1996) *Data Collection and Analysis.* London: Sage and The Open University.

Thyer, B. A. (1994) *Successful Publishing in Scholarly Journals.* (Survival Skills for Scholars Series) Thousand Oaks: Sage.

Turabian, K. L. (1982) *A Manual for Writers of Research Papers, Theses and Dissertations.* Oxford: Heinemann. (Although there isn't a later edition of the British version, the American version, *Manual for Writers of Term Papers, Theses and Dissertations,* published by the University of Chicago Press is now in its 6th edition (1996).)

Wheeler, S. (1999) Convergent technologies in distance learning delivery, *Tech Trends,* 43(5): 19.

Index

THE STUDENT'S GUIDE TO RESEARCH ETHICS

Paul Oliver

This new title examines the ethical issues and questions which occur in university and professional research. The book helps both beginner and experienced researchers to identify ethical issues when they are conducting research, and attempt to resolve those issues.

- Examines ethical issues which arise throughout research, from the design stage through to data collection and analysis
- Investigates topical issues including consent, confidentiality, ethical questions in the dissemination of research
- Discusses ethical theories and how these may be applied towards resolving ethical problems
- Provides examples of ethical dilemmas and case studies throughout the text

Insightful, wide-ranging and accessible, this title is an invaluable tool for both undergraduate and postgraduate students and professionals who research as part of their job.

Contents

192pp   0 335 21087 2 (Paperback)   0 335 21088 0 (Hardback)

WRITING AT UNIVERSITY
A GUIDE FOR STUDENTS
Phyllis Creme and Mary R. Lea

- What is expected of you in university writing?
- What can you do to develop and build confidence in your writing?
- How can you address the variety of written assignments you will encounter in your studies?

Writing at University is a student writing guide with a difference. It provides a deeper understanding of what writing at university is all about, with useful methods and approaches to give you more control over your academic writing.

The book explores both traditional essay and other kinds of writing that you will need to do as part of your studies. You are encouraged to build upon your existing abilities as a writer through applying practical tasks to your own work.

The second edition of this best-selling title has been completely updated with new coverage of report writing, learning journals, electronic writing and using the internet.

This book is an essential tool for anyone who wants to improve their writing skills at university or FE colleges, including both undergraduates and post-graduate students. It is key reading for students in courses that require essay, report, or dissertation writing and for students returning to study. It is also an invaluable resource for academic staff who want to support students with their writing.

Contents
You and university writing – First thoughts on writing assignments – Writing for different courses – Beginning with the title – Reading as part of writing – Organizing and shaping your writing – Putting yourself into your academic writing – Putting it together – Completing the assignment and preparing for next time – Using different kinds of writing – Using learning journals and other exploratory writing – References – Index.

160pp   0 335 21325 1 (Paperback)

THE STUDENT'S GUIDE TO EXAM SUCCESS

Eileen Tracy

Exams frighten almost everyone.

Fear of failure (and fear of success) can inhibit learning. Students will always perform better if they have the necessary emotional resources in the run-up to their exams.

Many study books fail to deliver what they promise: techniques alone do not necessarily boost exam performance. To work effectively, study advice has to take account of the variety of attitudes students have to the prospect of being assessed. These determine how successfully they adopt and develop study strategies for exam success.

In addition to fundamental student skills such as timetabling, note-taking, memorising, research, use of the internet, essay-writing and exam technique, *The Student's Guide to Exam Success* offers ground-breaking advice on developing emotional strength in response to the increasingly heavy demands that are made on students in the modern world. It offers a variety of strategies which will help students to:

- Develop self-awareness
- Find out how to stop procrastinating and worrying about results, and start to enjoy their work
- Learn about the dangers of swotting
- Develop the necessary confidence to handle reading lists, coursework, presentations and practicals
- Learn to deal with tutors, lecturers and examiners

Contents

Preface – Introduction – Part one: States of mind for success – Clear your head – Healthy body, healthy mind – Part two: Techniques for success – Lay solid study foundations – Remember, remember – Use resources wisely – Plan for success – Master your exams – Appendices – Bibliography – Index.

192pp   0 335 20726 X (Paperback)   0 335 20727 8 (Hardback)